"Women should read *Divided Lives* and take heart, men should read it and take note." —*Entertainment Weekly*

"A riveting read." —*Publishers Weekly*

"Groundbreaking." —*Chicago Sun-Times*

"An eye-opening study. Walsh shows us three women who are willing to cut the baloney and tell all . . . she shed[s] new light on why conventional journalism misses the real story of women's lives." —*San Francisco Chronicle*

"Clear-eyed and compassionate . . . Every woman will find herself in some measure in these pages." —*Times-Picayune*

"I ripped through it in an evening . . . Because the book is well written, it's easy to read. Because the women were frank and open about their lives, it's compelling . . . Read Elsa Walsh's book. I'll bet I'm not the only one who will close it and mutter, 'It wasn't supposed to be like this.' " —*Gannett News Service*

"A captivating portrait of three extraordinary individuals." —*Seattle Post-Intelligencer*

"Invaluable service . . . These tales are gripping, outrageous, and vividly drawn. Walsh is masterful." —*Cleveland Plain Dealer*

"By shining her investigative light into the crevices of [these women's] lives, Walsh creates three distinct narratives that are as intimate as they are objective. After all, if these women's lives are complex, divided, and at times fractured, what does that mean for the rest of us?" —*People*

"Elsa Walsh's fine new book finally puts a public face on this deeply personal struggle." —*lo News*

DIVIDED
LIVES

DIVIDED LIVES

The
Public and Private
Struggles of
Three American
Women

Elsa Walsh

ANCHOR BOOKS
DOUBLEDAY

NEW YORK LONDON TORONTO SYDNEY AUCKLAND

An Anchor Book

PUBLISHED BY DOUBLEDAY

a division of Bantam Doubleday Dell Publishing Group, Inc.
1540 Broadway, New York, New York 10036

Anchor Books, Doubleday, and the portrayal of an anchor
are trademarks of Doubleday, a division of Bantam Doubleday Dell
Publishing Group, Inc.

Divided Lives was originally published
in hardcover by Simon & Schuster in 1995.

Library of Congress Cataloging-in-Publication Data
Walsh, Elsa.
Divided lives : the public and private struggles of three American
women / Elsa Walsh. — 1st Anchor Books trade pbk. ed.
p.   cm.
Originally published: New York : Simon & Schuster, c1995.
1. Women—United States—Biography.   2. Vieira, Meredith.
3. Worby, Rachael.   4. Estabrook, Alison.   I. Title.
[CT3260.W35   1996]
920.72'0973—dc20   96-7647
                                                    CIP

ISBN 0-385-48447-X

1   3   5   7   9   10   8   6   4   2

For my mother and my father,
Mary and Redmond Walsh,
and for Bob

Contents

A Note to Readers

There was a time in the years after college when I refused, foolishly I now believe, to read any fiction written by men. I had had enough of the desires and ambitions of the women of Charles Dickens and F. Scott Fitzgerald, women who resembled no one I knew. To friends who recommended a male author, regardless of how renowned the classic, I declared I had spent enough time reading men. How could I appreciate Dickens's *Bleak House* when his heroine, who eagerly expects to marry one man, finds her fiancé has substituted a new man—a man she uncritically, even happily, agrees to marry on the spot? What a waste of time, I said, throwing down the book. I had met the image of woman as created by men and decided to reject it.

I was in my early twenties then, and had moved to Washington, D.C., to begin work as a journalist, but also to make a life for myself, I see now. I had no interest in marrying, or having children. I was anxious about my life, and thought if I found a feminine voice, someone who could craft women and their lives and could speak my interior language, I might find a story of my own. I was seeking guidance, perhaps a road map, on how a woman could live her life. With ferocious intensity, I turned to the fiction of Doris Lessing and Virginia Woolf, Joan Didion and Sylvia Plath.

But if I devoured fiction by women, I often found their autobiographies insufficiently honest or intimate. With few exceptions, it was as if nothing had changed since Woolf remarked that "very few women yet have written truthful autobiographies." Their real history, Woolf said, was "hidden either by silence, or flourishes and orna-ments that amount to silence." Biographies and memoirs seemed equally devoid of reality as my friends or I knew it. The world presented in these books was a place where women almost always were happy, accepting, and grate-ful. They rarely felt frustrated by their children or their husbands, and the good things that befell them came providentially. I began to hate the word "luck" when used by a woman. Although I admired Eudora Welty greatly as a writer, I could not finish her memoir, *One Writer's Beginnings*, because it seemed too optimistic. I could not overcome my feeling that Welty was putting one over on me and perhaps also on herself. When she wrote, "I wished to be not effaced but invisible," I thought she had succeeded. The irony was not lost on me that it was a man, Lytton Strachey, who turned con-vention on its head to describe Florence Nightingale's fierceness and determination in his portrayal of her in *Eminent Victorians*. Why did women not want to write about their private anguish, their secret pain—the honest personal writing I craved?

It was as if women in their own books viewed admissions of pain, anger, or confusion—or even just telling the true story about their roles as wives and mothers and friends—as betrayals of one of their central responsibilities as women. They seemed to have taken a blood oath to present the family as the font of all virtue and goodness. But it was no wonder. The rare writer who broke the taboo was met with scorn and shock, as poet and essayist Adrienne Rich found out when she wrote in *Of Woman Born* that women sometimes hate their infants. It so "shocked the women who were its first reviewers that the book was denied much of the publicity and exposure" it deserved, reported Carolyn G. Heilbrun in her remarkable book *Writing a Woman's Life.* Even Virginia Woolf confided privately in a letter that she had held back her anger in *A Room of One's Own* because she feared the work would be dismissed: "How personal, so will they say, rubbing their hands with glee, women always are; I even hear them as I write." Woolf's unmitigated scorn at a woman's plight did not emerge in her writing until she passed her 50th birthday and wrote "Three Guineas," an angry attack that compared the treatment of women to the making of war.

Yet it was these pieces of personal anger and private shame that always captivated me most. I can still remember as if it were yesterday the surprise, and then almost furtive comfort, I felt when I first came across Joan Didion's essay "In the Islands," one of the last in her collection *The White Album.* Expecting a hypnotic description of flora and fauna, I had settled in for a fluid read. Instead I had stopped dead before I reached the end of the first page. For there in the last sentence of the second paragraph was this: "We are here on this island in the middle of the Pacific in lieu of filing for divorce." I must have read that sentence a dozen times before moving on. It was not that I took prurient pleasure in Didion's pain, but that I felt I was reading something honest.

I continued my search through other nonfiction books about women. Many I found relied on polemical or academic arguments; others drew superficial portraits of the women discussed and offered pop-psychology prescriptions. Those that attempted to incorporate the voices of real women relied on so many subjects that depth and context were missing. Simone de Beauvoir's *The Second Sex*, published in this country in 1953, and Betty Friedan's *The Feminine Mystique* (1963), as well as Kate Millett's *Sexual Politics* (1970) and Germaine Greer's *The Female Eunuch* (1972), had altered the public debate about women, but I and women of my generation had come of age in a different era and were living under different circumstances. The arguments of *The Feminine Mystique*, in particular, seemed obvious and dated.

Later books focused on topics like the gender gap and discrimination, or debated feminist academic theory. Yet the dense and laborious prose typical of these books often made them completely inaccessible to all but the most determined reader. The language in Elizabeth Fox-Genovese's well-received *Feminism Without Illusions* is typical: "This book offers a critique of feminism's complicity in and acceptance of individualism—or rather of its contemporary atomized version that replaces the early and glorious recognition of the claims of the individual against the state with the celebration of egotism and the denial or indefensible reduction of the just claims of the community." The rich, discrete, individual lives of women were lost in the bigger theoretical debates. Even the professor who recommended Fox-Genovese's book to me suggested that I skip to the last chapter because it was the "most interesting." There Fox-Genovese abandons her academic turgidity and provides a personal account of her life as a woman. Yet the alternative for women—superficial self-help books filled with homilies and formulas—was equally unsatisfying. In the end, I found few answers on the bookshelf to the basic questions of how real women—as opposed to characters invented for the sake of argument—lived their lives, the questions that my friends and I talked about all the time but no one seemed to have examined in detail. The innermost lives of women had been left to the editors of *Cosmopolitan* or books that focused just on marriage, sex, beauty, or the language barriers between men and women. *The Cinderella Complex* and *Women Who Love Too Much*, prescriptive books that focused on women's relationships with men, come to mind.

During my period of research for this book, the debate about feminism, somewhat dormant and derided for much of the 1980s, reignited. Anita Hill and Clarence Thomas, Hillary Clinton, the date-rape trials of William Kennedy Smith and Mike Tyson, all stoked the fires and demonstrated that "the woman question" was not dead. Books and essays about feminism, pro and con, surfaced to widespread attention, generating fresh discussion about the legacy of the women's movement and creating what appeared to be a new generation of spokeswomen for it. Susan Faludi, the author of the bestselling *Backlash*, and Naomi Wolf, author of *The Beauty Myth* and then later *Fire with Fire*, appeared regularly in newspaper and magazine articles and on television, talking about the state of women today. Faludi was by far the most effective of the new spokeswomen. Marshaling an impressive amount of evidence and binding it with a strong ideological glue, she presented a cogent case that women had yet to achieve true equality because of a concerted effort to undermine the gains of women's liberation. Wolf argued in her first book, I believe much less artfully yet more emphatically, that male institutions created a beauty myth to "checkmate power at every level in individual women's lives." Both seemed to provide useful starting points for discussion, and Faludi, in particular, provided a framework for future battles in the legislature and the workplace.

As I began my own research, I found that women were looking not for more experts on their lives, but for flesh-and-blood stories that did not conform to the neat configurations of theories or social critiques. They wanted to hear about the full fabric of a woman's life from a personal point of view that validated their own experiences, and confirmed that others shared the internal conflicts that constantly left them feeling frustrated and guilty, regardless of their financial or professional successes. "Write this down," a psychologist who kept an office at home told me one morning after several interruptions from her children, who supposedly were being watched by a nanny. "Nothing works best," she said. "Whatever you do is less than perfect."

"Why do we keep doing this?" another woman asked me one day, after I had been interviewing her for over a year. She held an important management position in a political organization, and I had been steered to her as a "success" story. "Why do we all carry on when we're so miserable inside and this society is not responding, or it's responding so slowly? Most women work the same kind of schedules that their male counterparts do and have to work even harder, if anything. It's amazing to me that we just go on and on leaving our children every day and feeling guilty. It's as if we're powerless to change things."

I did not have to travel far for other examples of frustration. A few months after I began my research for this book, I was chatting with a married couple, close friends, when the conversation took a sudden turn. I had asked the woman why she had quit her job four years earlier. Her face tightened as she described the agony she had felt each morning as she and her husband left their home and their toddler son for their respective jobs. The husband was a writer and she worked for a foundation. Recounting the feeling as if it were yesterday, she described how the anxiety mounted as she would sit at her desk, imagining her son in terrible jeopardy. But he, she said, staring at her husband, never worried.

A bewildered look crossed her husband's face. He agreed, but was uncertain what, if anything, he had done wrong. They had a healthy son and someone they trusted watching him in their home. They had well-paying jobs they loved and a nice apartment, he said in an almost pleading tone. He thought they had the perfect setup. The woman bit her lip and the two left within minutes. These were two intelligent, well-intentioned, and good-hearted people. He was not a chauvinist. She considered herself a feminist. When I later asked her why she had been so upset, she responded wearily, "If only I could find the internal thread, then I would not have to make so many choices."

It was an exploration of this interior pull and tug of women's lives that I thought was lacking in the nonfiction literature. This is not to say that men do not experience similar ambivalence; they do and are probably thrown off stride as women are, though they might reveal it to the outside world in different ways. But the conflicts invariably seemed more emotional, frightening, daunting, and even devastating for women than men.

The battle beneath the surface of a woman's life, the beliefs and the fears that she brought to her decisions, had gone curiously unrecorded. This was the book that I wanted to write. I thought that by focusing a reporter's lens on women's lives as they are lived very much from the inside, I could shed some light on what seemed to be preventing women from living their lives smoothly—a phrase I choose intentionally to underscore the unevenness I sensed. By looking in depth at only a handful of women and presenting my material in the form of stories about individual women, I thought I could help bridge the gap in women's literature between the rich storytelling tradition found in fiction written most often by women and the distant and, in my view, ultimately unsatisfactory, bloodless tone that characterizes much of nonfiction written about women or for women.

I used as a starting point a running dialogue my friends and I had conducted over the past decade about the women we knew. We periodically gave each other updates, inevitably describing what the woman in question was or was not happy about. As I reviewed those conversations, I recognized that I almost always divided my description of a woman's life into three categories, as if they were the sum total of her experience: her job, her relationship with a man, and her relationship with her

children. A recent recounting of a meeting with a journalist friend was typical. I had described the woman as
bursting with excitement about her job, her eyes grown
wide with wild accounts of stories chased. But I had said
she became sullen when the conversation turned to her
husband, and her voice had shrunk with embarrassment
at questions about her child. Her friends, she knew, gossiped about the limited time she spent at home. "I am a
bad mother," she had said to me. Yet when I thought
about that conversation I knew I was leaving out areas of
that woman's life that perhaps were equally important,
and gave her satisfaction.

To this woman I knew, for example, friendships were
vital, a source of intimacy and affection, a safe harbor for
the sharing of secrets, the confession of vulnerabilities.
This journalist friend would fly back from assignments,
often rearranging interviews, to make it to her twice-a-
month lunches with her closest women friends. I had another married friend who reserved a night each week for
dinner with women friends, dates she depended on
heavily to compare notes on feelings and experiences
she felt her husband would not understand. Another
friend despaired as much about the change in her closest
friendship following the recent birth of her child as
about the change in her relationship with her husband.

Nearly every woman I knew, especially those with
children, complained about having little or no time for
herself. Searching for even an unencumbered 15 minutes
at the end of the workday took on the status of the quest
for the Holy Grail. But time alone seemed to be the first
thing women discarded in days crammed to accommodate everyone else. "You don't own any of your own
time. That's a given," one working mother told me. "You

come in with none. You go out with none." Reserving a portion of the day or the week for herself seemed selfish, yet women who did—whether it was a Saturday afternoon at home to read or just poke around, or an hour swimming laps—often were calmer and able to cope better with their other demands than women who did not.

A woman's home—or, more generally, her sense of place—could not be forgotten either. Homes or cities or special locales were nests, places of dominion and security. An unmarried friend with a powerful job was radiant when she described a new summer home. "It's my spoiled child," she said laughing. In my own life, a weekend house my husband and I built together by the Chesapeake Bay has given me grounding and serenity, a sense of completion. Missing out on a weekend there brings a feeling of life not being fully lived.

These three additional measures of a woman's life—time with friends, time by oneself, and a sense of place or home—could be as critical to a sense of well-being as the other three. But as I reviewed these it dawned on me that I was missing what might be the most important measure of a woman's well-being: her sense of independence or autonomy. I am not referring here to the traditional definitions of independence: financial security, career advancement, or self-enhancement. I am thinking more of a core self that is developed only by defining beliefs and values, choosing a destiny and establishing life goals. It is what Lily Briscoe, the artist in Virginia Woolf's *To the Lighthouse*, finally achieved after years of "groping toward the central idea of her life," as Carolyn Heilbrun described it.

This sense of self often strengthens or weakens the other areas of a woman's life. But it is, perhaps, the most difficult state to achieve for a woman because women have been accustomed to defining themselves according to others' needs, and have not devoted the time or attention needed to examine their own. Women who have a clear sense of self and purpose, however, can better weather instability in the other areas: the breakup of a marriage, the departure of children, the change in a friendship, the loss of a job, the move to a new home, or paucity of time for self.

I was not looking to write a prescriptive book that would seek a new formula to help women maximize the happiness or harmony in their lives; nor was I seeking a magic formula. I simply thought if I divided a woman's life into seven areas and then looked at them separately and then together I would have found a useful tool to examine more deeply the layers of a woman's life. I expected that after I completed my research the seven areas would have served the purpose of a painter's pencil—to sketch outlines on the new canvas—crucial to the drafting of the painting but invisible in the final work.

As my reporting progressed, however, the seven measures began to emerge more prominently rather than recede. Not only did they provide a useful technique for assessing the important aspects of a woman's life, they also provided a structure for zeroing in on the sources of satisfaction or discontent, allowing problem areas to be isolated, the roots probed (separating a self-created problem from an external one), and its ramifications laid out. Once isolated, problems could be attacked more easily and analyzed more fully, and strategies for change devised.

• • •

When I began compiling lists of women to interview, I limited myself primarily to women in their late thirties and early forties, beneficiaries of the women's movement, whose age meant they either had children or had seriously considered the question of whether to become mothers. Women in their twenties still had the luxury of believing in limitless options, while older women found fewer options. Women in their late 30s and early 40s were at the crossroads of a still evolving generation, and taking a snapshot of their lives at this moment would tell more about the nature of the dilemma and the conflicts than a look at women of the generation ahead or behind them.

I did not want to study activists in the women's movement because I did not want to engage in theory or polemical arguments, although I did want to interview women who felt they had integrated into their lives some of the movement's central tenets. Work outside of the home needed to be, or to have been once, a central part of their lives. I compiled my own lists of women and I trolled for suggestions from other people. I always asked the women I interviewed for names of others. After months of canvassing dozens of women, I narrowed my list first to a dozen, then seven, then five, and finally three. To travel deep I could not travel broad; larger truths would come from the exploration of individual lives. Throughout my interviews and my writing, however, I tried to incorporate the insights and experiences shared by the dozens of other women I interviewed along the way.

In the end, I deliberately chose women who enjoyed all the advantages of wealth, education, and opportunity, and who had broken through barriers traditionally viewed as male. My three subjects are television journalist Meredith Vieira, conductor and first lady of West Virginia Rachael Worby, and breast surgeon Dr. Alison Estabrook. They allowed me to describe their innermost conflicts and fears. Each was facing a major change during the time we talked. These hypersuccessful women had the intellects, resources, and opportunities to make informed decisions about their lives. Relatively free of some of life's routine burdens, they seemed to have the luxury of choice and the best shot at achieving happiness and balance in their lives. They are women who, indeed, seemed to be having it all. This is precisely why I chose them. If these women of privilege were finding the challenges of balancing their lives a struggle, then that said something important about the condition of women generally and made it worth exploring just what is not working.

I had learned from reporting other in-depth stories that people often are not and cannot be entirely candid or truthful in the first few interviews. They may not themselves fully understand what they think and feel, and in addition, the interviewer may not yet know enough to have asked the right questions. Compounding the natural obstacles in this instance was the fact that women tend to be reticent about such topics as the ambivalence they might feel toward their children or husbands. I stopped asking women if they were happy with their marriages after several women reflexively answered yes and then proceeded to describe how miserable they were. To overcome these obstacles, I decided to establish a routine of regular interviews with each of my subjects, spanning more than a two-year period. That way I could peel back the layers, and reach closer to what is often hidden or unexpressed in women's lives.

There were some false starts. A year into my interviews with one woman she revealed that she had gone into therapy during her daughter's infancy because she deeply resented being a mother. Our conversation, she said, was "off the record" and I could not use the information. She would not budge, despite my pleas that this was exactly the kind of hidden information that I wanted to bring to light in the book because it would help other women see they were not monsters if they shared similar sentiments. I dropped her as a subject.

Using the seven measures, I began to discover over the course of my interviews that a woman's initial explanation for a particular emotion later gave way to a very different account. For example, I found that a number of women who first attributed their slackening in a career to the birth of a child often acknowledged later that they had in fact begun to feel ambivalent about their jobs well before the pregnancy. Scratching off another layer, I saw these same powerful and highly competent women grow pale as they described work environments at odds with their own values, where political alliances often count more than merit. Some women also expected to enjoy breaks in their careers in a way men never did, and having a child provided both an escape (however temporary) from the job and an opportunity to feel more altruistic.

Other hidden explanations surfaced as the interview process continued. When I examined the spheres of home and children, I was consistently surprised in my interviews by women's willingness, almost without exception, to shoulder the bulk of the domestic and child responsibilities, even though they were sharing the responsibilities of the workplace. What was especially surprising was how vocally they complained about the unfair burden placed upon them, while nonetheless doing little to force a change. In *The Feminine Mystique*, Friedan envisioned that home responsibilities would decrease and be shared with men as large numbers of women entered the workforce. But Arlie Hochschild, in her 1989 book, *The Second Shift: Working Parents and the Revolution at Home,* reported that most working women performed at least two-thirds of the daily household tasks.

As I talked to women, it was clear that a woman's typical response—that it was easier for her to do it herself than fight with her husband—was too simple. Women had bought into the ideal of the conventional family with a woman at the center of the home in a big way. Educated and middle-class women seemed only to have raised the standards. Women's expectations of themselves as mothers seemed to be as rigid as ever, maybe more so. They were driving themselves crazy with their idealized version of perfect mothering, hauling their children from one lesson to the next, leaving no time for themselves. Men were not sharing the burden, but women were letting them get away with it for more complicated reasons. I regularly heard women say they did not have their husbands perform certain household tasks because they did lousy jobs. One woman I interviewed complained her husband had no ability to substitute at the grocery store, meaning she had to do the grocery shopping. If she included broccoli on her list, she said, he would bring home broccoli even if it was yellow with age. But when I asked how many times she had sent him before giving up, she said only twice. Was she afraid of losing control of her domain?

The women interviewed who had families uniformly

expressed increasing guilt and anxiety as they became more successful in the workplace. It was as if they were being yanked dramatically between two great forces. These women often wanted to continue advancing in a career, yet they believed they had a primary responsibility to their children. Men seemed to be able to separate their work lives from their home lives, yet very few women succeeded in keeping at bay a home problem while at work. One approach was not necessarily "better," but a woman's approach certainly had a more noticeable drag on her work. If the tension became too great, a woman tended to pull back or break away from her career. At the same time, each woman in this book saw herself as struggling with painful work issues, from the male-dominated elite world of classical music to the machismo-ridden culture of surgeons.

Each chapter focuses on one of the three women, and each is told as a narrative in an effort to show the life as a whole. The narratives are, in large part, autobiographical and told from the perspective of the woman; they represent the subject's version of the truth and reflect her interior reactions. But I also have interviewed many of the people who were prominent in my subjects' lives, to check facts like dates and places, and in some instances to give a fuller range of views, where particular skepticism might be in order, or to serve as reflectors illuminating my subject's life. The stories, as a result, are not fully inclusive and, most likely, would read differently if told from another perspective. But, again, that is the point.

I also concentrate on a limited period of crisis and change in each of the women's lives for the same reasons I eventually narrowed my subjects to three. I thought greater truths could be learned about a woman's decision making and her sense of self from an examination of an intense period of demand and conflict.

I often left my interviews feeling disturbed emotionally and intellectually. All of the women were willing to undergo a rigorous, at times fierce, examination, and some wept as they attempted to sort out how they had reached certain stages in their lives. Despite all the gains, they lived divided lives, unable to integrate the parts and overwhelmed with frustration and guilt. In particular, I am still haunted by the memory of Meredith Vieira sitting at her kitchen table sobbing, wondering why she seemed not to be able to get anything right. The choices and pain that lay behind the answer to that question are at the heart of this book, and, I believe, many a woman's struggle.

Meredith's STORY

Meredith Vieira walked toward the office of the president of CBS News. A correspondent on the network's hip prime-time magazine show *West 57th*, Meredith, 35, was nine months pregnant with her first child and scheduled to start a six-month maternity leave the next day. She had a natural, fresh look rare for television, and her brown hair, high cheekbones, and full lips drew comparisons to the actress Isabella Rossellini, though this day she felt huge and unattractive, having outgrown everything except a two-piece blue maternity suit and a purple one. She was apprehensive about the meeting.

She'd hoped to slip out of the office unnoticed, but David Burke, the president of the news division of CBS, had asked her to stop by at 10 A.M. It was February 3, 1989. Though she liked him, Meredith also knew that he was a serious and formal man, not given to frivolous gestures, and she suspected he wanted to talk about work. Her four-year contract was almost up, and, as one of the network's up and coming stars, she expected he would try to pressure her to make another commitment before she left. Work, however, was not high on her list at the moment. She'd had three difficult miscarriages in the past two years, and all she wanted to do was go home, take a break, be a mom, a wife—and reassess the direction of her life. The pace of the last four years had been a killer: she'd been on the road almost constantly, away for up to three weeks at a time. Plus television news seemed increasingly schlocky and celebrity driven, at odds with her view of the news. She was beginning to wonder whether she should leave TV altogether to do something useful, like train as a social worker or write children's books. But she felt uncertain, and she didn't feel like discussing her future, even with someone like Burke, who had encouraged her to have a family and seemed to be one of the few people at the network comfortable talking about kids.

She eased into a chair in his office, arching her back to compensate for the extra weight. She'd eaten a quart of Ben and Jerry's ice cream a day in an effort to try anything to make this baby stick, and gained 60 pounds in the process. "You've been great," she said, trying to keep the conversation on her ground in the warm and coaxing voice that had helped her land her first job sight unseen as a radio announcer just out of Tufts University. Any traces of the harsh accent of her native Rhode Island had been erased by years at a tony all-girls Quaker academy, Lincoln School.

Burke was a lanky man, whose shy and remote demeanor had earned him the nickname the "headmaster," but he'd always been taken by Meredith and he smiled at her gratitude. A fan of hers for years, he had tried desperately to hire her while he still was working at ABC, and his opinion of her had only grown since his arrival at CBS. He thought she was an extraordinary reporter and a graceful writer, a skill rare for on-air reporters, and she was a good person, kind and refreshingly unpretentious in a field populated by demanding divas. When he talked about Meredith he used descriptions like "a person of some gravitas," "serious," and "special"—adjectives he used to distinguish her from her peers in television. Burke had spent the better part of his career in public service and believed firmly that the networks had a public trust to protect. Though Meredith had done her share of celebrity-type stories on *West 57th,* she'd also gone to Ethiopia to report on starvation and toured the underbelly of Chicago with a 9-year-old boy for a report on hunger as seen through the eyes of a child. The body and soul of her work were significant, compassionate, and unique.

He'd heard she was tired of *West 57th.* Did she have any ideas about what she might like to do when she returned?

"I'm not sure. Can we talk again in six months?" she asked anxiously.

Burke pressed. He did not want to lose Meredith to the other networks, which undoubtedly would woo her. He reminded her of the high esteem in which she was held at CBS. Howard Stringer, his boss as president of CBS's Broadcast Group, gushed all the time about her, in *Esquire* magazine calling her a "wonderful role model for every modern woman you could think of." Critics loved her, too. Tom Shales, the TV critic for *The Washington*

Post, had raved, "Even among network wonder women such as Diane Sawyer, Maria Shriver and Kathleen Sullivan, Vieira seems exceptionally wonderful."

Burke was willing to discuss any job, he said. "Would you like to do *60 Minutes?*" he asked.

Burke did not need to mention that a few days earlier, on January 31, 1989, word had leaked that Diane Sawyer, the great blonde hope of CBS and the first female correspondent on *60 Minutes,* the pioneering Sunday news-magazine show, was defecting to ABC. The move had shocked the media world and stirred up stories suggesting CBS's dominance in network news had finally come to an end.

Burke said he and Don Hewitt, the brash executive producer and creator of *60 Minutes,* thought Sawyer's departure had provided an opportunity to inject some young blood into the show's otherwise aging lineup and introduce a new generation of correspondents (Mike Wallace was 70; Harry Reasoner, 65; Morley Safer, 57; and Ed Bradley, 47). Meredith immediately had come to mind. Hewitt had also suggested Jane Wallace, a former correspondent on *West 57th,* but Wallace had been in disfavor with CBS executives since leaving the network. Meredith was the only real choice.

Meredith paused, as if stricken. "It's the one broadcast I really want to do," she told Burke. "But can I go have my baby and then talk about it?"

Though she knew it was irrational, Meredith could feel her anger rising, and she wanted to leave before it became apparent. She thought she had made it clear for such a long time that she just wanted to go away and have this baby, take a leave. She wanted to work less, not more. Now the network was dangling in front of her the one carrot that she might not be able to resist. She wasn't prepared to reshuffle her future plans right then and there, but she knew her own weakness. She was driven and this was the one job she had coveted since she began her TV career in 1977 in Providence, Rhode Island. She could still recall watching *60 Minutes* one night when she was barely a year out of college and telling herself, "I'm going to be on that show." Everything she'd done since then had been directed toward reaching this point— moving to Chicago when the network asked, returning to New York to join *West 57th* against her wishes, putting off having a child. She came from a family of overachievers. Her father, now deceased, had been a Harvard-educated doctor and worked into his 80s. One brother had followed in the father's footsteps, and two others were lawyers. Meredith, the youngest child and the only girl, had been prodded by her mother to do even more, and, helped along by opportunities created in television by the women's movement, she hadn't yet disappointed. She was furious, not just with Burke and CBS, but with the situation, with the timing, and mostly with herself. Turning down the job would be nearly impossible, however much she protested.

Meredith's hesitation surprised Burke. *60 Minutes* was the most popular prime-time show in the history of television, a piece of Americana, and the aspiration of nearly every broadcast journalist. Only six correspondents had worked on the show since its 1968 premiere, and thirty million or so viewers tuned in each week, giving it the kind of impact that could make a government agency or company change policy almost overnight. Its star correspondents were among the most recognizable faces in the country. That Meredith did not jump at the job impressed Burke and reinforced his respect for her. She had her own set of priorities.

"Think about it," he urged her.

"Am I already selling out my child?" Meredith asked herself, rushing out of his office. She felt trapped in a classic dilemma, one that might have seemed like a good story if it were not her own life: Woman delays having children to build her career, but has succeeded so well that what should be the peak of her career and personal life is really a collision about to happen. She returned to her office and packed up a few things to take home.

In their small Upper West Side brownstone apartment, Meredith described Burke's offer to her husband, Richard Cohen, a former producer at CBS. She was sitting in the living room on their old sofa, threadbare from the cats' clawing. The furniture had a college hand-me-down look, typical of the low-key life they preferred. Meredith broke into tears.

"What's the problem?" Richard asked, perplexed. Five years her senior and a tall man with a raspy voice, Richard had few illusions about CBS. He'd been one of its best news producers, but also one of its most vocal inhouse critics, until he had left a year earlier after executives tired of his acerbic public criticisms of the news division. He'd written "From Murrow to Mediocrity"— a manifesto questioning the direction of CBS News under its new owners—that ran on the editorial page of *The New York Times* in March 1987 under his name and Dan Rather's, and had been quoted in a news article criticizing Rather's performance in a testy live debate with then Vice-President George Bush. When he was removed shortly as the senior producer in charge of campaign coverage, he quit the network. Still, Richard was independent-minded and he respected *60 Minutes* and Hewitt, who had offered him a producer's job after he left the *Evening News*. When Richard turned it down, saying he thought he needed to get away from CBS, Hewitt replied tartly, "This isn't CBS. This is *60 Minutes*."

If Meredith took the job, Richard told her, she would have an opportunity to tackle stories that mattered in a forum that made a difference. Although he viewed Meredith's work at *West 57th* as significant, he detested *West 57th*'s glitzy packaging and jazzy music, viewing it as a sorry symbol of CBS's decline into the gutter of tabloid journalism. Meredith was better than that, her talents and standards more suited to a show like *60 Minutes*.

Meredith continued to weep as she tried to explain her confusion. She felt inarticulate, unable to describe her own mixed emotions. She knew her inner turmoil was in part hormonal, caused by her pregnancy, but it was also rooted in real concerns: taking the job would mean getting back on airplanes and a tremendous amount of time away from home. She had waited too long, gone through too much pain with the miscarriages, to hand off her baby to someone else. Taking the job would also mean instant fame, and she wasn't sure if she wanted that. She was simultaneously attracted and repelled by the idea.

"If you don't want to do it, don't do it," Richard said, always practical.

She'd been able to say no to CBS before when they first tried to recruit her while she was still at their local affiliate in New York City in 1980. She thought she wasn't ready then and thought she might fail. But now she had had a dozen years of training. She was professionally prepared. Who knew when, or even if, this opportunity might come around again? Only two correspondents had ever left *60 Minutes* in its twenty-year history. Correspondents took these jobs for life. Also, if she saw her work as an advocate to change the world, as she often said, then she would never have a better medium in television than *60 Minutes.* With the show's track record, a story on *60 Minutes* had a rare, almost unmatched power to define issues.

"This will work if you want to do it," her husband said. The baby would not be small forever. "Maybe you can work part time," he added. If she traveled less and had the flexibility to work out of the house, it could be manageable. He would not be traveling much because he was editing a documentary in town, and he looked forward to playing Mr. Mom for a while. He'd spent a lot of years overseas with CBS and had had a full life living what he called "the adventure." He did not want that anymore.

Two distinct voices battled within her: Don't do it, it's a major mistake, one voice said. You've got to do it, the other shouted.

Six days later, on February 9, 1989, Benjamin Edwin Cohen was delivered by cesarean section. Flowers started arriving from CBS executives. Meredith noted wryly that they were not the carnation-daisy kind of grouping she'd seen arriving for others at the hospital. These were big bouquets of roses. Political statements.

Phone calls followed, including one from Mike Wallace, *60 Minutes*'s biggest gun. Wallace pitched the show to her. When Meredith was noncommittal, Wallace, who'd given his life to the show, spending half his time on the road, sounded stunned.

The pressure intensified when she met Burke for lunch three weeks after Ben's birth. She continued to equivocate, but this time she raised Richard's suggestion about working part time and sometimes out of the house. Burke, who hoped Meredith would take the job, said he thought they might be able to accommodate her, but he needed to check with Hewitt. He urged her to make a decision soon. "We cannot hold the job open forever," he said. Meredith replied that she wanted to take the full six months of her maternity leave before making a decision. Maybe it would all just go away.

Although Meredith knew in her heart she was going to say yes, she continued to put off the decision. As the weeks went by, her lawyer, Washington attorney Robert Barnett, reported that Burke had called him to say *60 Minutes* would "love to have her part time." He told her that Burke had said, "She is very important to CBS. We don't want her to leave." Still Meredith hesitated. She had to justify it to herself. If she talked about it enough, someone might provide an argument that would erase her guilt, or persuade her not to do it. Her heart warned her: "You've struggled too long to have this child. It was so hard to get pregnant. You can't continue to put your life on hold for your job." Her ambition countered: "You're a fool. This is the pinnacle. You have to take this. You've always wanted it."

No one seemed to understand her reluctance. Most surprisingly, her women producer friends showed little empathy. One friend had been walking with Meredith, who was holding Ben in a sling, when Meredith confessed she was struggling with the decision. The producer stopped dead in her tracks. "You have to take this job," she said, looking at Meredith as if she were rejecting life itself. It was a once-in-a-lifetime shot. Most new mothers turned up on the morning shows, the maternity graveyard. Was she crazy? Meredith realized it was pointless to continue the conversation. Meredith almost shook with confusion, but there was no way this friend could understand. She did not have children. When Meredith looked at Ben she felt overwhelmed with love, an indescribable fullness unlike anything she had ever felt in her life.

She asked another good friend, a producer, to meet for lunch at a seafood restaurant on the Upper West Side. This friend also had no children, but Meredith had talked with her endlessly about wanting to mother this child, not just have him to dispatch to a baby-sitter, and the friend had seemed to empathize. Sitting in the restaurant, Meredith reviewed her contradictory feelings, frequently looking over at Ben in his stroller.

Usually, the producer friend tended to listen rather than give Meredith advice—there were enough people always doing that with Meredith—but this time she told Meredith she thought she could manage. At *West 57th*, everyone had bent over backward to accommodate Meredith's efforts to have a family; *60 Minutes* couldn't be all that different. "This is a real opportunity," she said. "You should consider it."

Later, Meredith and Richard continued the debate. What should she do? she asked him repeatedly. Even though they had a pact not to interfere with each other's career—criticize, yes, but dictate, no—on some level she did not want to take responsibility for this decision and was looking to him to take responsibility for the choice.

"You have to decide this yourself," he told her. But she asked him to go through the pros and cons with her again. On the positive side, he reiterated his belief that *60 Minutes* was the best magazine, with an opportunity to work on stories that made a difference. On the negative side, it might disrupt them as a family. The correspondents on *60 Minutes* lived on junk food and planes, and were away from home about 100 days a year.

Traveling created psychic as well as physical distance in a marriage, and Meredith attributed a lot of the ups and downs in their three-year marriage to her extended absences. She had reduced her traveling significantly during this last pregnancy because her executive producer at *West 57th,* Andy Lack, had encouraged her not to fly, fearing she might have another miscarriage. The extra nights at home had greatly improved their relationship, giving it a consistency and normalcy it had lacked. She'd always thought the best part of a relationship was the quiet time, not the once-a-week passionate meetings, when you tried so hard to have fun. She felt that she and Richard had finally become a family. She worried about risking that.

Whatever her decision, Richard warned, if she entered the job with mixed feelings she would be setting herself up for failure. *60 Minutes* required a 100 percent effort.

In mid-April, Barnett, Meredith's lawyer, said CBS was willing to accede to most of her requests. Burke wanted to close the deal. Meredith was in a prime negotiating position. Roone Arledge, the president of ABC News, was wooing her, and nothing in television made executives more competitive than trying to keep a star talent. Barnett said CBS was willing to offer her a four-year contract that would require her to produce roughly half the number of stories required of the other correspondents—about ten—for the first two years. For the next two, she would be expected to produce the full load. Her salary would start at about $450,000 and would be reviewed when she went full time. Most of the other correspondents earned more than a million a year.

In practical terms, Meredith calculated, she had struck a good deal. She would work a full day every day, but travel only once or twice a month and control when and where she would go. She would have a team of producers, probably five of the best in the business, assigned just to her. The pace and workload probably would be more manageable and maybe even lighter than it was at *West 57th*, since *60 Minutes* had a bigger budget and a more experienced staff.

Near the end of April, she spoke with Hewitt and agreed to meet him and his deputy for lunch. As she dressed that morning, she decided to take Ben with her. She had not yet hired a regular baby-sitter, and negotiations at CBS were typically low key. More importantly, though, she thought she needed Ben at her side. She was worried that if Hewitt changed his mind about the part-time arrangement, she might cave and agree to a full-time schedule. "Meredith Vieira, TV journalist" was a larger part of her identity than she liked to admit. This was her first meeting to discuss the job with Hewitt, who could be disarmingly persuasive, infectiously enthusiastic. If she clutched Ben's hand and looked down at him, she would be reminded that there was something more important than her job. That was the statement she hoped she would make. She was throwing the ball back into Hewitt's court, shoving the diaper pail in his nose, forcing him to accept the agreement on her terms. She wasn't giving any of it up.

Hewitt picked her up after a dental appointment, and they drove to the Tavern on the Green, a festive restaurant in the middle of Central Park. Although the weather was chilly, the mood inside was cheerful. Bright-colored Venetian-like chandeliers hung from above, and floor-to-ceiling windows looked out onto huge topiary animals. She sensed that Ben's presence had thrown Hewitt, but he reacted sweetly. "Does he need a bassinet?" he asked.

"It's only lunch," she said, laughing. "He can sit in the stroller."

Hewitt had loved the story she had done for *West 57th* about the nine-year-old Chicago boy and hunger, and he talked about similar kinds of stories she might be able to do for *60 Minutes.* Hewitt liked to say that the stories on *60 Minutes* were "little morality plays, only they're real." The same small cast of correspondents were the protagonists.

The discussion quickly turned to her schedule request. He reiterated that he had no problem with her working part time for the first couple of years; Steve Kroft, a colleague of Meredith's at *West 57th,* planned to join the show at the same time, giving them an extra person, and together they could report what a full-time correspondent would. Hewitt also said he was comfortable with her working from home, as long as her producers didn't mind.

Meredith was relieved. The meeting was going more smoothly than she had expected. Maybe it could work.

"You've got to realize that Harry Reasoner will probably be retiring, and at that point I will need you full time," Hewitt added. Reasoner had been in declining health since undergoing surgery for lung cancer.

Near the end of the lunch, Meredith voiced a reservation. "You know, I might have to come back a year later and say this is not working," she said. Her qualification, however, had the ring of an afterthought, not a serious disqualifier, and Hewitt did not pursue it.

She felt uneasy as she left the restaurant. Hewitt had agreed to everything she asked. But was she writing off her child for her own ambitions? She hadn't even mentioned that she wanted more children. How would she fit that in? But then Meredith slipped into her Pollyana mode. She pledged to herself that she would never be away from home for more than two nights. When I'm not traveling, I can work from home, using a computer and fax. With a few adjustments everything will work out, she told herself.

Back at the office, news that Meredith had brought Ben to the negotiations raced through the building. Lack, her executive producer at *West 57th*, could not believe it. What psychological reason had prompted her to do such a stupid thing? he wondered. Lack had done everything he could to make sure she had her baby and the kind of family life she wanted, even when other colleagues had criticized him severely for keeping her off the road in a season when *West 57th* was fighting for its life. He'd do it again for Meredith because he believed he had a moral obligation to make those kinds of adjustments. Pregnancy, in his view, should be treated like an illness in a career. This was part of the contract people made with others in the workplace. But he knew he was of a different generation from Hewitt, 66, and others who worked at *60 Minutes*, and that might not bode well for Meredith. At *West 57th*, everyone was having children, and their spouses worked. Kids were in the office frequently. At *60 Minutes*, all the children were grown-up and the show was the be-all and end-all for the people there. That single-mindedness, Lack thought, probably was the one reason for the show's extraordinary success. He knew Meredith wanted more kids. How were Hewitt and the others going to react to that?

On April 23 Richard was unexpectedly hospitalized for nearly a week. He had multiple sclerosis (MS), a disease that attacks the nervous system. Though he was legally blind and could not drive as a result of the illness, it did not normally affect him or his ability to work—he could read, for example. His father also had it, but he had so few noticeable symptoms that he did not tell Richard about it until Richard was in his twenties and his father suggested he undergo testing. Only a limited number are incapacitated by MS and many live normal lives with only minor disabilities, but MS is unpredictable, with no known cure, and the setback scared Meredith, who tended to envision the worst. It prompted renewed worry about her contract and salary at CBS. If something happened to him, she thought, she might end up being the sole source of income for the family. She felt a responsibility to earn as much as she could.

On May 11, 1989, CBS announced that Meredith and Steve Kroft had joined *60 Minutes*. The press release stated that Meredith would not start work until September, the end of her maternity leave.

• • •

Even though she had promised herself she would concentrate on Ben in the remaining months of her maternity leave, Meredith immediately started churning about
story ideas. Less than two weeks after the announcement, she called Paul and Holly Fine, a husband and
wife producing team based in Washington. The Fines
were among the show's best producers, with a reputation for doing the compassionate kind of stories Meredith liked. Meredith asked them to consider updating her
story about Anthony, the poor Chicago boy.

They agreed to look at the old tape, and on June 9 she
traveled to Washington, arriving at the Fines' office in
the afternoon. Still breast-feeding every two hours, she
had brought Ben with her reflexively, but for a moment
she stepped outside of herself. Maybe this was a stupid
mistake, she worried, imagining the Fines' perspective.
They could be offended or think she was being preten-
tious, demanding attention, and when Ben spit up she
was horrified. Once no one flinched she relaxed. The
Fines had two children, ages 11 and 16, and the conversation quickly turned to kids, working, and traveling.

"Was it bad that this job came when it did?" Holly
asked. She'd heard about Meredith's miscarriages, and
her experience with other friends who had trouble conceiving was they became enormously protective once
they had a child.

"I couldn't turn it down," Meredith said. She knew the
travel would be tough, she continued, but "it was a once-
in-a-lifetime thing."

After Meredith left, Holly wondered how Meredith
was going to cope. Meredith was as likable as colleagues

had said she would be; her presence filled the room, and she had an appealing natural style in blue jeans, a white T-shirt, and navy jacket, with absolutely no makeup. But it was obvious to Holly that Meredith was conflicted and hadn't really made a choice about whom she wanted to be. She seemed to have one foot inside *60 Minutes* and one foot out. How was she going to manage? Seeing Meredith brought back her own pain when she had to travel when her children were young. Even though Holly had drastically cut back her travel to about once every three or four months, much less than Meredith's proposed schedule, something happened without fail. When she returned home after being trapped by a snowstorm in St. Louis for two days, for example, her babysitter bolted from the house and ran down the street in three inches of snow, screaming, "I'm not taking this anymore. I'm leaving." Holly had just sat down and cried. "This isn't worth it," she told herself. And no matter what Meredith might be telling herself about it getting easier as her child aged, it was only going to get harder. She knew that from her own experience. She and Paul had started traveling extensively again for a story during one six-month period when her children were nine and four, and she always came home to kids out of control, a complete mess. She tried to solve it by getting a better baby-sitter, but that was not the solution. Being at home was. Travel takes a toll on kids. Period. Children's needs don't disappear, they just change and grow.

Holly concluded that Meredith had to be using *60 Minutes* as a stepping-stone, an opportunity to build up fame and exposure to land a spot with a big salary as an anchor on a local station. It had to be. Otherwise, it was unfathomable.

• • •

Over the next two months Hewitt called regularly, urging Meredith to come into the office to start putting together a staff. The calls weren't unreasonable, just not what she had imagined for the first few months of motherhood. He tracked her down in Nags Head, North Carolina, on Father's Day. She reached him at his home in the Hamptons.

"Okay, listen, Don," she said. "I'm on maternity leave but I'll come in. But I've got to bring Ben."

Sitting in her office later, she looked over at Ben and felt guilty. This was not good for him, and it wasn't good for her. It was almost impossible to get work done with Ben there.

"Meredith, you have to work this out better with the baby," her assistant, Maureen Cashin, told her after she had brought Ben in several times. Cashin, 32, had followed Meredith from *West 57th,* and adored her, which sometimes meant delivering advice Meredith did not want to hear. Cashin had already deflected a number of snide comments about the baby's presence from other people at *60 Minutes.*

"I know. I know," Meredith replied. She was looking for a baby-sitter.

After Meredith disrupted another week in August with staff lunches and picking out office furniture, she wrote angrily on her calendar for August 14, "Left to go on maternity leave again. This time stick to it!" She directed Cashin to underline "MV out of the office" for the next two weeks. That meant she was serious, and she stuck to it until September 5, when she reluctantly checked into a spa at Hewitt's suggestion to tone up for a week and shed the extra pounds she'd gained from her pregnancy.

The show was in full production schedule when she arrived in mid-September, and two weeks later Meredith was packing her bags for her first overnight trip for a story, about the first deaf president of Gallaudet University, a college for hearing-impaired students in Washington, D.C. She had a heavy interview schedule, and the Fines, the producers on the story, had asked her to come down a night early to prepare. They had already finished the bulk of the research and reporting, as was the norm at *60 Minutes*, where producers drove the show. Outnumbering the correspondents by a factor of about four, producers at *60 Minutes* typically came up with a story idea and then executed it by gathering extensive background information, completing most of the reporting and then scheduling on-camera interviews for the correspondents. It was not unusual for a producer to have finished three-quarters of the work by the time a correspondent arrived.

As Meredith kissed Ben good-bye, she started to cry. "Meredith, I could understand if you're going to Ethiopia, but you're going to Washington," Richard said wearily. Meredith knew he had a point. She was making this into a lot more than it needed to be. She now had a full-time baby-sitter—though the baby-sitter did not live in the house—and Richard was in town, working temporarily with Bill Moyers, and he loved taking Ben into the office. There would be two adults in her absence, not to mention Moyers and his staff.

Crossing the gangway to the shuttle bound for Washington, she told herself, "Now the treadmill begins for real." But as she continued down the aisle, her dueling selves reared up once more. One moment she swelled with pride, wanting people to recognize her accomplishment. She had reached the top. But before she could enjoy that feeling, her other side sharply chastised her insecurity. "I am a turncoat," she said, strapping herself into her seat. "I am trading my child for celebrity." That night in her room at the Grand Hotel she picked up the phone and called home. After the sixth call, Richard finally told Meredith to stop crying, to stop calling, and to go to bed.

Meredith always had an ability to focus intensely when she was working, and the next day her worries submerged temporarily while she interviewed King Jordan, the college president. But by midafternoon her jacket barely fit because her breasts had become so engorged with milk. She wanted to get home.

On the return flight, Meredith realized she had thought about what kind of mother she wanted to be on an intellectual level, but she had not had a sufficient understanding of the emotional undercurrent that would tug at her constantly. Even though she felt she and Richard had acted responsibly as parents, she still felt she owed Ben something more than the truncated version of mothering she had given him since his birth. Her intention to work out of the house had come to nought; after just a few days her assistant, Cashin, had started reporting to her that if she was not there by ten Hewitt came barreling down the hall, demanding to know where she was. Though Hewitt had assured her in their negotiations that he did not care where she worked, it was clear her absences disturbed him. If she was to have any chance of succeeding, she realized she needed to be in the office, a presence. Everyone else at *60 Minutes* seemed to be there all the time, making her absences even more noticable. Few of the women producers had children, and those who did did not talk about them. She was disappointed in herself that she did not force the issue, but she wanted this to work.

Underlying much of Meredith's ambivalence was the firm conviction that she wanted to be a different kind of parent from her mother, whose entire life revolved around her children. Meredith thought her mother had been too available, tending to her every need and those of her three brothers, and in the process living out her ambitions vicariously through her children, and particularly through her only daughter. She hadn't seemed happy or satisfied in her role. She was always telling Meredith she had to get a job. "Never rely on anyone. You need to be self-sufficient. You need to do it yourself." Annoyed at the hovering, Meredith had wished her mother would herself get a job and had sometimes muttered disparagingly under her breath, "All you do is sit around." Meredith had told herself then, "I want to be something. I want an adventure." Now that she had achieved that goal, Meredith still flinched with discomfort watching her mother become most animated with pride when a stranger remarked, "Oh, you're Meredith Vieira's mother," or a friend mentioned she had read a story about Meredith. When Meredith told her mother about her first pregnancy, she reacted coldly, and the seeming indifference crushed Meredith, who attributed it to her mother's fears about the pregnancy's effect on Meredith's career. She did not want to find herself like that 20 years from now.

In contrast, her father worked long hours, tending primarily to the Portuguese community, and rarely made it home in time for the family dinner, but when he did he regaled the family with interesting stories. Though both parents brought a European formality to their relationships, Meredith idolized her father and yearned for his affection. Tears still came to her eyes when she recalled the day, at age nine, she worked up the courage to tell her father she loved him. After practicing in the basement, she ascended the stairs to the kitchen, where he was sitting on a kitchen chair watching a football game on television. "I love you," she said. He did not answer. As an adult she could speculate that he might not have heard her, but as a girl the silence was devastating. She never said the words again to him until she was a young adult.

Meredith wanted her children to have breathing room to develop for themselves, but she also wanted to be available and affectionate, always warm. Quantity time, not just quality, was crucial. When she became pregnant, she thought she had worked it out better than her mother. She could spend time with her child, and have a job. She wasn't going to be trapped, she had thought.

Not long after returning from Washington, Meredith met with Hewitt and the Fines to review the tapes of her interview with King Jordan in the *60 Minutes* screening room. The Fines had warned Meredith the screening would not be easy. Hewitt, who compared himself to a magazine editor, liked to mold correspondents to a *60 Minutes* style, one that took time, practice, and a very thick skin to acquire. His withering judgment had led some people to call the screening room the screaming room.

Hewitt took a seat in one of the navy-blue theater-like chairs, propping his feet on the table in his customary position. Meredith sat nearby with her legs dangling over the side of a chair; she was wearing gray leggings and red boots. Hewitt, who tended to speak in rapid spurts, started in right away. She should have challenged Jordan's argument that a deaf person can do anything.

"People in the audience might not agree with this," he said. "You have to approach an interview with their skepticism."

Meredith disagreed. Jordan was right.

Hewitt had little tolerance for advocacy journalism, and he couldn't stand someone pushing an ideological agenda. "You've really got to question that. You have to be less believing," Hewitt said, becoming more emphatic. His infamously short patience was starting to surface. She needed to be tougher. "You'll have a better interview," he said.

Hewitt next addressed the camera angles. Paul Fine had not shot Jordan's face close up, like most *60 Minutes* pieces. What was going on here? Meredith pointed out testily that, although Jordan was speaking, he had been using sign-language for deaf people who might be watching. *60 Minutes* was close-captioned for hearing-impaired people, Hewitt said. Go back and reinterview Jordan, he said. Ask tougher questions, and shoot it closer.

Even though they thought they had prepared Meredith, the Fines could see that she was unnerved by the harshness of Hewitt's reaction. Hewitt, however, was right about Meredith's questions. She had been too soft.

Meredith left the room, the insecurities that lingered right below the surface tapped. She'd swept the Emmys the week before she came to *60 Minutes*, winning an almost unheard-of four awards for her work on *West 57th*, and she knew she had a unique and effective style. But she also was aware that she had a lot to learn if she was to become the equal of the other correspondents. Morley was a better writer, Ed a more polished performer and interviewer, and Mike the kind of in-your-face investigative reporter she would never be. Even before coming to *60 Minutes*, she had felt plagued by a feeling of being exposed as a fraud, of being discovered that she could not really pull it off. She knew enough about the human psyche to understand that her fear was typical of overachievers, but the knowledge didn't ease her anxieties. She was always the first to criticize her own work, chiding herself after nearly every interview that she had not gone far enough or there was no story. Hewitt's criticisms reinforced her fears, and not just about her competence.

Meredith also felt ambivalent about her looks, and it was obvious that Hewitt's standard for comparison was not the men but Diane Sawyer, his blonde goddess. Countless people had warned Meredith that Hewitt worshiped Sawyer, and even though he had made a number of nasty comments about her since her departure, those were more the comments of a spurned lover than a true critic, they said. Sawyer radiated the kind of glamorous star quality that Hewitt liked to cultivate for his correspondents. She appeared regularly in the gossip columns and in the company of the elite, and had that kind of cashmere-sweater-slung-over-the shoulder look that he preferred. Sawyer had an extraordinary ability to make people feel like geniuses—and Hewitt had been no exception. Anyone who followed Sawyer was going to have a very tough time. That she and Meredith were so different exacerbated what was already a difficult situation. Meredith liked to come to the office in jeans and a sweater rather than a suit on days she was not filming, and she shunned parties, preferring the company of old friends and journalism colleagues. She always had felt more comfortable as earth mother than siren. Her appearance had been a constant sore point since her arrival. Hewitt had complained regularly to Cashin and others that neither her hair nor clothes were sophisticated enough. He'd even given Cashin the names of contacts with the designers Calvin Klein and Donna Karan. "You have got to get her some clothes," he told Cashin, who repeated the conversations to Meredith.

Though Cashin thought Meredith looked beautiful in anything, she began monitoring Meredith's clothing. She wanted to make this work. She considered Meredith her closest friend, and was appreciative of all the gestures, large and small, Meredith had made for her over the years, from bringing Cashin with her to *60 Minutes* to taking Cashin and not one of the heavies to lunch at the Manhattan Ocean Club on Meredith's first day of work. Cashin knew their closeness puzzled others at *60 Minutes*, where a social distance between a correspondent and an assistant was expected, but Meredith never altered her behavior. Other assistants confided their envy to Cashin, telling her she had the best job of any of them. She agreed, having seen the abuse some of the other correspondents and senior people heaped on the support staff.

"You cannot wear that anymore," Cashin told her one morning shortly after Hewitt had stopped by to complain. Meredith reacted defensively, "My job is to tell a story." But she calmed down and acknowledged that Hewitt had a point. Television was a visual medium, and looking good was the price of earning her kind of salary. She agreed to go to the Donna Karan and Calvin Klein studios.

"When you go on the road, then you don't have to say what goes with this and this," Cashin explained after picking out basic pieces to make sure they all went together. When the bill arrived, Meredith almost hyperventilated. "I could buy something for Ben," she protested.

Meredith, Cashin concluded, was almost congenitally incapable of doing something for herself without guilt, so Cashin would have to do it for her. If she saw a blouse or nice pair of shoes, she bought them for Meredith. If Meredith came in with her hair tied back, Cashin approached her before Hewitt could. "Meredith, you cannot come in with your hair in a ponytail again," Cashin said.

But Cashin sensed Meredith's clothes were the least of her problems. This was not *West 57th Street* anymore, where everyone was like family and Meredith had seemed so carefree that she once told Cashin she wanted to give away her company health insurance to someone who really needed it. Meredith had been nutty and fun then, always ready to laugh. But those days were long past. *60 Minutes* was fiercely competitive, and about as far from collegial as Cashin could imagine.

"Can't the baby-sitter do that?" one senior staffer complained impatiently when Cashin explained that Meredith was at the pediatrician with Ben.

"Why doesn't she have live-in help?" another asked.

Cashin felt as if she were translating a foreign language, patiently explaining that it was important to Meredith to take her newborn child to the doctor or that she did not want live-in help because she felt she and Richard already had enough intrusions on their privacy. But she also felt they had a point, and Cashin gently suggested to Meredith that it might ease some of her burden if she had a baby-sitter living in her house. Then she wouldn't have to rush home to deal with the series of calamities that seemed to come along with having a new baby.

"I did not have this child to have a baby-sitter raise it," Meredith responded. She also knew herself well enough to know that if she hired someone to live in the house she would treat her like family, and she already had her plate full.

Meredith also had a secret fear that she shared with very few people. Meredith was worried Richard might have a sudden flare-up of his illness and drop Ben, or fall. One of the symptoms of MS is temporary weakness, which can cause someone to fumble. She had confided in one friend that he had banged Ben's head into some pots hanging from the ceiling once. If she had been there, that would not have happened, she said. The friend thought Meredith was overreacting; any parent could do the same. But Meredith was determined to get home every single night before the baby-sitter left.

When she was without a baby-sitter in January because her Irish baby-sitter was refused reentry into the country after a trip home to Ireland, Meredith brought Ben with her to California for two days. Suzanne St. Pierre, the producer, had no objections. They had only one interview scheduled, and the interview was going to be in a place hospitable to children.

Meredith's defensiveness masked the terror she felt about her status. She'd gotten off to a slower start than she had hoped and by early January had not yet had a story air. Until she did, she knew she would feel like a nonentity. Steve Kroft had broadcast four pieces by mid-December, a real leg up on her, even though she told herself that he had started earlier. Once she compensated by acting overly aggressive in an interview with a spokeswoman for a New York City private employment agency. Afterwards, the spokeswoman asked what it was like working at *60 Minutes*. It's hard, Meredith responded, because she was "competing with people like Mike Wallace." Another company representative, listening to the interview, mumbled sarcastically under her breath, "You have nothing to worry about there."

She had five pieces under development—King Jordan; the trade in surplus zoo animals; racial discrimination in the employment agency; Christians who had hidden Jews from the Nazis; and corruption in the criminal-justice system in Texas. She was traveling regularly. She'd made ten trips in her first four months. But the *60 Min-*

utes style was more difficult than she had expected. She had not yet mastered putting herself at the forefront of a story, as Hewitt preferred, and Hewitt had sent her back to reshoot some segments, complaining about her narration.

Suzanne St. Pierre, a producer who was working with Meredith on the Christian-rescuers piece, assured her that all correspondents took a year or two to grow into the *60 Minutes* style. But Meredith knew she wasn't just any correspondent—she was young and with a baby—and the expectations of herself and others were enormous. There had been tremendous media interest in her as the woman who replaced Diane and the correspondent with a baby. She wanted to be a good role model for women in similar positions. "I think we all feel we're establishing important precedents for working mothers," she had just told *Working Mother* magazine, describing her efforts to combine a high-profile, high-pressure job with motherhood.

But privately she wondered what she was trying to prove, and at what cost? To demonstrate she could do her work, she had laid down laws for herself, like never being late on a script. Because she was a perfectionist in her writing, however, that meant staying up until all hours to finish scripts, poring over transcripts, looking for that one quote to make the piece better, or rewriting a sentence a dozen times to find the right cadence. But she also wanted to be with Ben—all the time—and she slipped out of the office early or left the house later than planned in the mornings. Her temporary location in Walter Cronkite's old office, a large, quiet space away from the corridor of *60 Minutes* offices, made her comings and goings easier than they would have been had her office been in eyesight of Hewitt, but she still felt un-comfortable. When she was at the office she thought she should be home. When she was home, she thought she should be at the office. She felt divided, unable to come to any peace about sharing herself, and each day was getting tougher.

On January 21, her first piece ran—a heart-wrenching exposé of the fate of surplus zoo animals—and Cashin threw a party for Meredith at Cashin's house. Next, in mid-February, came her employment-agency story, which prompted a state investigation. For the first time, some of the internal pressure dissipated.

But not all. Interviewed in February by a *Newsday* reporter writing a story about her debut, she admitted that her thoughts more often veered to Ben than to the next big story. "You have to check yourself every day to make sure your value system is intact. Look, it's just TV—it's very good TV. And yeah, this office was occupied by a legend, but it's still just an office on West 57th Street," she told the reporter, referring to Walter Cronkite. The reporter described her as a "puzzling mixture of elation and unhappiness—even anger—over her new-found status." She made a crack to David Letterman when she appeared on his show that something he said made her breasts lactate. Cashin cringed.

Don Hewitt said nothing to her about the interviews, though he had a long history of hypersensitivity to anything that cast even the slightest shadow on his broadcast. Hewitt was obsessed with ratings. One producer pulled her aside to suggest she cool the family angle. Another, Holly Fine, thought Meredith's directness and frankness were what made Meredith wonderful, but she told her it was a mistake to say she put her child ahead of the show. Others might feel the same way, but they had the good sense not to say it. One of the cardinal rules of *60 Minutes* was that nothing was more important in life than *60 Minutes.*

Meredith knew her comments were risky, but she barreled ahead. Her family was her priority, and she wanted to remind Hewitt and her colleagues that her choices not to hire a live-in sitter and to continue devoting time to Ben were deliberate. She had another audience, too. Herself. People stopped her in the street. She had been on Johnny Carson. She met important figures. She had been honored by *Esquire* magazine at a black-tie party at the Plaza Hotel as one of their "Women We Love." She knew how easy it was to get swept away by that, to start believing she was some big deal. She did not want that to happen to her.

To limit her time away from home, Meredith learned she could cram four days of interviews into two if she interviewed late into the night and hardly broke for meals. She caught late-evening flights that returned her to New York at dawn. But even with the abbreviated trips her departures were becoming more painful rather than less, accompanied always by her own tears and Ben's. She was traumatized when he became hysterical at the airport as she was boarding the plane to Los Angeles to be on the Carson show.

Early that winter she faced her toughest test. The Romanian government had fallen in December 1989 and stories were filtering out about crowded mass orphanages overflowing with thousands of unwanted children with physical and mental disabilities. Meredith was immediately drawn to the story because of the children angle. She asked Hewitt if she could go. The story already had been on the *Evening News*, Hewitt pointed out, making it old news. But Meredith persisted and Jane Stone, a producer she had brought with her from *West 57th*, found a former Romanian broadcaster now living in New York who agreed to return with a camera crew to show how journalists like herself had helped to cover up the horrors of the former regime.

There was no way she could report this story in less than a week, and she told Stone and Cashin she was thinking of taking Ben with her. If she were away for more than three days, Meredith insisted, "he's not going to remember who I am." Cashin was certain this was a bad idea, but she knew once Meredith got an idea into her head it was hard to dislodge. Medicine might be unavailable in Romania if Ben became ill, Cashin finally pointed out. Maybe she should not go at all then, Meredith said. If I say family is my priority, why am I doing this?

Richard, who tended to agree that extended absences were harmful, encouraged her to make the trip. She should see Eastern Europe—he had—and it was an important story. She told herself she could help the children. This was her pattern when it came to breaking self-set rules. Cashin had seen it too many times to be surprised. If the story was heartbreaking and could engender some good, she usually went. Meredith had traveled to North Carolina the weekend of December 16, for example, to interview the daughter of a couple who had hidden Jewish children to save them from the Holocaust, despite another personal rule not to travel on weekends. But before she left she needed to get everything in order. She wrote a will.

On March 23, she flew to Romania—without Ben. Once there, Meredith did not immediately go to the orphanages. She knew that she needed to prepare herself emotionally. Her hotel was bleak and dingy. Still breast-feeding, Meredith had packed a portable breast pump to squeeze out the milk from her breasts every morning and night to reduce the painful swelling and to ensure she could continue lactating when she returned home. Ben was 13 months, and she could have stopped breast-feeding months ago, but doctors said it was better for an infant's health to breast-feed as long as possible, and it was one of the few remaining links to Ben that was uniquely hers. But the breast pump didn't work, forcing Meredith to pull at her breasts as if she were milking a cow as she lay in bed. The first tugs were always the most painful, releasing a tremendous flow of milk onto the sheets. She never quite mastered the technique, however, and one night collapsed in bed without releasing her milk. She awoke the next morning with breasts almost solid as a rock, pulsing with pain.

Near the end of the week, Meredith finally made her way to an orphanage. The rooms were cold and damp as if all the floors were made of concrete, and the children, mostly toddlers and infants, were filthy. Herded like animals and tied to metal cribs that resembled prison cells, some children had only scraps of clothing. A number of children were infected with the AIDS virus, and the wails of crying children filled the rooms. Tears streamed down her face. Desperate beautiful faces and hands, reaching out, hungry. There were no toys or blankets, there was no color. One moment she was furious with the women watching the infants, the next deeply sorry for them because they too were desperate, overwhelmed by the numbers, with almost no food and few supplies.

"I can't do these stories anymore," she thought. "All I do is fall apart."

Meredith reached to pick up a child. She was a little afraid of the drooling and spitting, fearing he might have AIDS and could infect her, but she had to provide some comfort. She then picked up a beautiful baby girl. Her body was ravaged by AIDS, nearly reduced to a cadaver, but Meredith thought the little face was breathtaking. She kept thinking of Ben and how lucky she was to have a child who was safe and healthy. "There but for the grace of God go I," she whispered to herself. Having a child made it so much harder to see children suffering in any way. Meredith later turned to Jane Stone and told her she wanted to look into adopting the little girl and bringing her home. She had so much. Ben had so much.

"Are you serious?" Jane asked. Meredith often had a problem maintaining the journalistic distance that most reporters brought to stories. Meredith still kept in touch with Anthony, the Chicago boy she had profiled for her *West 57th* story on hunger, and had set up a trust fund for him, with donations that had poured in after the story aired. She'd wanted to bring him home with her, too. Jane pointed out that adopting a child in Romania was a bureaucratic nightmare, which would be compounded by the difficulty of caring for a dying child. "Would you really do this?" Jane asked.

"I would if Richard wouldn't kill me," Meredith said

quietly. Richard always reminded Meredith that she had to be willing to pay the price of her good intentions. She knew she could not take a sick baby on now. But it was so awful. Later that night she called Richard from her hotel to make sure he brought Ben with him to the airport when she returned.

Eight days after leaving, Meredith's plane arrived in New York on March 31. After clearing customs, she raced over to Richard and Ben, extending her arms. Ben turned his head away. Meredith fell apart, convinced he was punishing her for her absence.

Richard thought she was overreacting. Ben was not old enough for that kind of thought process. "Kids will be kids," he said, trying to explain away Ben's coolness and ease her anxiety, but she was not buying it. He could see she was a mess. But he was beginning to tire of the constant emotional turmoil which was wearing all of them down, and creating dissonance in their own relationship.

When she later described the scene to Cashin, she started to cry. "It's not anything you did. This is the way kids react," Cashin insisted. Meredith seemed shattered, and would not accept that explanation. "I shouldn't have done this," Meredith said. "The rules I set for myself have been totally broken." She now had to make her child remember that she was his mother, she said.

"Meredith, you can't be everything to everybody," Cashin said. "You're not the only parent here. You have to share this job." She pointed out that Meredith was making it difficult for Richard to be a partner by insisting on being responsible for everything. That is not fair, Cashin said gently. This was the excessive Meredith who brought an intensity, a need to do everything, to all her relationships, including hers with Cashin. It was what made Cashin love Meredith, but it also drove her crazy.

Meredith brushed aside Cashin's arguments, insisting that she was now going to enforce rigid restrictions on days she would travel. Cashin did not think Meredith was asking for anything big—Meredith had a right to a life—and she would do whatever she could to make Meredith's life reasonable, but she also knew fitting everything in was going to be difficult. Cashin would have to schedule everything to the nanosecond, and that didn't include the inevitable glitches or the delays caused by Meredith's proclivity to talk endlessly to people she interviewed. If someone mentioned to Meredith they had passed over Rhode Island in an airplane, Meredith would go into a long narrative about being raised there. She never breezed in and out, like other correspondents.

Meredith saw the incident as something more, however, something she did not like to admit, even to Richard, because it embarrassed her. Her travels were forcing her to cede the center of the family to him, and she did not like it. She wanted to be the emotional nucleus of the family, the primary nurturer. That was the way it was supposed to be. As a helpless infant Ben needed her, but she also needed him to need her. She had finally found someone who was going to love her unconditionally in a way she had never experienced. She desperately wanted to have a close mother-child relationship. She wasn't sure she wanted to share the relationship, however much she intellectually understood that it was important to include Richard. Although Ben's indifference at the airport was minor, it confirmed her deepest fears. The problem wasn't that the family did not function without her. It was that it functioned well enough. Maybe she was not as indispensable as she wanted to be.

To compensate, she tried making herself essential in other ways. She hadn't cared about a clean house before Ben was born, but now she cleaned obsessively, sometimes folding laundry and washing floors well past midnight. Richard stopped her one day in the midst of a fight and asked, "Does it ever occur to you to stop and be happy and give yourself a break? Give me a break?" He reminded her of the sign his mother kept near her chimney: "May this house be clean enough to be healthy and dirty enough to be happy."

Cashin saw it as part of a pattern. Meredith wouldn't go to the doctor with a sore throat unless someone screamed at her, yet she would exert endless energy on someone else's problem. When she came into the office fretting about a problem her dry cleaner had, insisting they do something, Cashin asked if she even knew the man's name. Meredith took better care of her cat than of herself.

Time for herself had gone out long ago, even though Meredith sometimes liked nothing more than to be by herself or just hang out, talking about girl stuff, without any responsibilities for anyone except for herself.

Just as Meredith was feeling overwhelmed that she could do nothing well enough, her fourth piece, "Thy Brother's Keeper," aired on April 15, 1990. Its appearance made her feel that maybe the hardship was worth it. Sitting in front of the ticking *60 Minutes* clock that opens each segment, Meredith introduced the piece that was a forerunner to the movie *Schindler's List:* " 'Thy Brother's Keeper' is a story about some courageous Europeans who risked their lives during World War II to save their friends and neighbors, and in many cases total strangers. The people they saved were Jews. The people who risked their lives to save them were Christians, Protestants and Catholics, Christians of every denomination. It is a story we frankly did not know too much about until we met a man who was determined the whole world should know this story. His name is Harold Schulweis, Rabbi Harold Schulweis of Los Angeles, and he tells Jewish congregations that it is not true that nobody cared and that when people read about the Holocaust generations from now they should know what he calls a spark in that darkness."

She had traveled to North Carolina, California, Philadelphia, and Florida for the story, and the piece included interviews with the Jewish children, now adults, who survived, as well as the rescuers and their children. At one point, she asked a survivor what he would have done had he been the one in a position to rescue a Jewish child. His rescuer had five children of her own living in the house, children who would have been hung from the balcony had she been caught.

"Should she have risked her family, do you think, for you and six other people?" Meredith asked.

"No, I don't think so," he responded. "I think it was— logically speaking it was irresponsible on her part. . . . This is not a human act. It's beyond that."

"What is it if it's not that?" Meredith asked softly.

"She's a saint, I think," he said. "It's beyond that. I wouldn't have done it."

"You know you wouldn't have?" Meredith pressed.

"No, I'm a normal person. Perhaps. . . . I could risk my own life, maybe, but to risk five children . . ."

This was why she had come to *60 Minutes*. While other news magazines breathlessly aired tabloidlike stories, her body of work so far had been compelling and serious. "Thy Brother's Keeper" eventually won an Emmy. The piece was characteristic of Meredith's style in other ways, too. She hated being at the center of a story and purposefully kept herself out of the piece. But that was atypical of the *60 Minutes* formula, which had correspondents showing up as many as 30 times—in about a quarter of the shots. Meredith appeared in "Thy Brother's Keeper" only eight times.

Five days after "Thy Brother's Keeper" aired, on April 20, Meredith flew to California to film a story about the nurses who worked on a hospital ward, at San Francisco General Hospital, dedicated exclusively to AIDS patients. Paul and Holly Fine, the producers, had asked Meredith to work with them on the piece because they knew they needed someone who would be sensitive and empathetic. Paul had already spent a week on the ward and the nurses were extremely protective of the patients, many of whom were in excruciating pain and in the messy last stages of dying, and wary of outsiders. The Fines' worst nightmare, like every *60 Minutes* producer's, was that one of the bigfoot correspondents would come in and undo the trust they had carefully built up. Meredith, Paul thought, was "real people," not a star. Also, one of Meredith's brothers was a doctor treating AIDS patients and she had expressed an earlier interest in the subject.

Meredith had agreed to spend about a week on the ward, even though it meant another long absence from home, because she knew if she wanted the patients and nurses to open up she needed to prove that she cared enough to spend the time. She was not, however, going to repeat the Romanian experience. She asked Cashin to book her two rooms at the Mark Hopkins Hotel. She was bringing Ben this time, and his nanny. She planned not to tell anyone at the office except Paul and Holly Fine.

"I have Ben here," she told them when she arrived, "so I'm not sure how long I can stay each day."

The Fines did not flinch. Holly suspected Meredith brought Ben as an escape in case the story became too emotionally difficult, as it undoubtedly would. But she also knew Meredith was nervous about leaving Ben at home for long stretches because of her fears about Richard's illness. Although she did not suggest his illness was an insurmountable problem, Holly saw it worried her. Traveling as a parent was tough enough without this kind of concern hanging overhead, and she and Paul were willing to do anything to make it easier for Meredith.

Paul explained to Meredith that they were not going to shoot any film the first few days, and he suggested she use the time to get to know the nurses and the patients. Some patients did not want to be filmed, and he showed her the names listed on a board, assuming she would avoid their rooms. Over the next couple of days, however, Paul noticed that Meredith, dressed simply in jeans and a navy-blue jacket, entered nearly every room, including those on the board, and that she had immediately disregarded her time restrictions, arriving every morning by 8 A.M. and staying all day. She was low-keyed and gentle.

But there was one patient Meredith was avoiding: a transsexual named Angel, with bleached yellow hair and dark roots, and extremely long fingernails. He was already near death, using a ventilator to breathe. He looked like a stereotypically bizarre San Francisco case, someone who would send a homophobic person running away down the street. Until she met his nurse, Meredith did not want to deal with him either.

"I've never thought of myself as a parent, but I do here," the nurse told Meredith, "and I find myself occasionally calling patients 'son' and I've never done that anywhere. But I can't help it. I feel like a mother."

"It's worth it?" Meredith asked, trembling visibly. "Worth it to say 'son' to somebody and watch him die?"

"Yes," the nurse answered. "I want them to know their life was meaningful and that I care and that people do care that they're sick."

Meredith walked to Angel's room and forced herself to enter. She asked him about the nurse's comments. "I feel like I'm nobody," he repeated. She felt ashamed of herself. She had been determined not to cry in front of the patients because she thought it would cheapen their suffering, but she broke down in Angel's room.

That night she picked up Ben and hugged him and told herself over and over again how lucky she was. She had him and she could do these kinds of stories.

The time with Ben, however, was short-lived. Three days after they returned from San Francisco, Meredith boarded another plane to California alone—this time for a story about an abusive high school coach. She was away for five days, breaking her rule again.

A little over a week later, one of Meredith's stories led the broadcast for the first time. "Anchorwoman," a story about a Romanian journalist, aired on May 13. Hewitt had called the piece "excellent" and described her narration as "first rate" in a memo he wrote her before it ran. Putting it first meant something else again. A story's position reflected Hewitt's preference. Maybe she was finally turning the corner.

Meredith was savoring her triumph the next day when Mike Wallace stormed into her office, ranting that he was disgusted with the piece. An imposing figure with a leathery face, Wallace was sometimes called the nation's prime-time prosecutor, and he showed little restraint in his attack on the story. It was an embarrassment, misleading, he exploded. He had received a letter from a friend who knew the journalist, claiming that Meredith had exaggerated the journalist's title. She was a correspondent, not an anchorwoman, and furthermore Meredith had made it seem as if she had left Romania yesterday, when in fact she had left years earlier. "How could you do this?" he screamed. "How could you air it?"

Meredith tried to answer calmly, a composure made difficult by the ferocity of his outburst. "I'm sorry you feel that way," she answered, not knowing what else to say as he turned on his heel and stomped out. He had ambushed her like one of the targets of his investigative pieces. Meredith became furious. Wallace's reaction was completely out of proportion to his complaint, and his treatment of her demeaning. She knew from Cashin that he had complained about her child-care arrangements, and she knew he didn't like Jane Stone, the producer of the segment. She pushed back from her desk and charged into his office, tears filling her eyes. But instead of rationally defending her work, explaining the decisions she had made, she was enraged—all emotion, barely articulate. She hardly heard what he said in response, if anything.

But even before she finished her own outburst, Meredith had second thoughts. Her crying was pathetic. Why hadn't she risen above her emotions and stood up for her work? Why hadn't she initially said instead, "Don't leave my office. I don't always like the things you do either."

One producer listened to Meredith's anguished description of Wallace's eruption and dismissed it as a temper tantrum designed to test Meredith's mettle. Wallace could be uncontrollably competitive, and he had a long history of personality clashes and struggles over stories with other correspondents and producers. At one point, he and Safer hadn't spoken for two years, and at another he and Ed hadn't spoken, either. Didn't she know that his style was to jump all over people, probing for weak spots? Her piece had run before his in the lineup, and that brought out his insecurities. Undermining her credibility put him back on top. Maybe he was even trying to toughen her up, the producer said. The mistakes, if they were that, were minor and unintentional. Forget about it, the producer counseled.

That advice, however, was easier in the telling than in the doing. Meredith knew if Wallace hated it Hewitt would not be far behind, because Mike often set the tone for Hewitt's reaction. Before the piece ran, Hewitt had been laudatory and had even balanced his customary criticism of her attire with some compliments as well in his memo. "I thought you looked sensational," in the red jacket and blue sweater in the interviews, he wrote to her in a memo, "but the outfit you wore on the street with Alina leaves a lot to be desired. . . . You just didn't look like the same class act that you looked like in the interview." That would all seem like minor criticism compared to what she was in store for now from Hewitt, she knew. Her suspicions were right. Hewitt let it be known that he was not pleased. Hewitt had made it clear before this piece that people in the halls were not buzzing about her stories; and in his eyes, invisibility was the kiss of death.

Would she ever fit in with the *60 Minutes* culture? Did she even want to? Everyone always seemed to be screaming and yelling up and down the hallway or running in and out of each other's office. It was either a confrontational or clubby atmosphere, and both were uncomfortable for her. She hated conflict and she didn't have time to socialize. To get home on time, she needed to close her door and work. But she could see that the job was more than hours working and that she had amplified her alienation by resisting repeated entreaties to move from Walter Cronkite's old office to "murderers row"—the corridor of offices where everyone else sat. Hewitt had been after her for quite some time to make the shift, but she had resisted.

Her time to brood was limited. She had another trip scheduled to California—her seventh in six months—as well as interviews in Baltimore and New Jersey with the actor Charles Dutton, who had turned his life around after a stint in prison.

To top it off, she and Richard were moving. Their apartment was too small for a family and they'd spent months looking before buying a large stone house with a yard about half an hour from the city in Westchester County. She had not wanted to move out of the city, but Richard thought the quality of life was not good for children. He was probably right, but she did not look forward to leaving Manhattan.

Meredith wanted to have more than one child and, given her history of three miscarriages, she thought she had little time. She was nearly 37. Who knew when she would conceive again and carry a baby to term? It had taken more than two years to conceive Ben. She was trying to get pregnant again. On Friday, July 6, Meredith called her doctor from a pay phone at the corner of 105th Street and West End Avenue to check on the results of a pregnancy test she had taken the previous day. The day was jammed. This was moving day, and she was leaving that night for Rome. Meredith had interviews for a profile on José Carreras, the Spanish tenor who had come back after a battle with cancer, and planned to attend his performance at the so-called "concert of the century" in Rome's open-air Caracalla Theater, along with Luciano Pavarotti and Placido Domingo. She was pregnant, her doctor said, but he saw no reason to postpone the trip. Her hormones were shooting through the roof, a good sign.

That night in the bathroom on the flight over, Meredith discovered she was bleeding, a possible indicator of a miscarriage. "It's nothing," she said, reminding herself that she had bled intermittently during her other pregnancies and that her hormone readings were great. She anxiously noted the bleeding in her calendar. Because of her earlier problems, she kept detailed records.

Meredith immediately slipped into bed at the hotel, telling the producer she felt like she had the flu and would prefer to lie in bed until her interviews. The spotting had turned into an intermittent flow, and she could think of nothing else, but she was determined not to tell the crew. The producer was not one of her regular team, and she did not want him to think she was holding up production because of some female problem. But even if she had felt comfortable with him, no one, she was sure, expected she would become pregnant again in the first year of a four-year contract. Cashin had repeated enough critical comments others had made for Meredith to know that her *60 Minutes* colleagues wouldn't throw a champagne celebration for her as they had at *West 57th*. Announcing she was pregnant here—and maybe miscarrying—would be disastrous. Alone in the hotel room, she probed herself for blood with sheets and sheets of toilet paper. The bleeding was not continuous. On one trip to the bathroom it had stopped. "Great," she sighed. The next time, however, she found a lot of blood. She called Richard. It was pointless to see a doctor. The bleeding was either insignificant or the end, but there was nothing anybody could do to save the baby. Experience had taught her that.

At the performance that night, she and the crew had been assigned some of the best seats in the house. Richard, who loved opera, would have killed to be there, but she barely heard the music—Pavarotti singing "Nessun Dorma" from *Turandot* and Domingo "E Lucevan le Stelle" from *Tosca*, the medley with "Maria" and "O Sole Mio." By this time she was certain something was seriously wrong. The next day the bleeding had become continuous. She'd arranged to interview all three tenors together. Though they couldn't have been nicer, they immediately slipped into their standard interview routine, a common dodge used by celebrities accustomed to interviews. With a lot of fortitude she could probably have chipped away the pat answers, but her concentration was shot.

An assistant producer, a young man she liked, pulled her aside. "Is everything okay?" he asked with a look of concern. She had to confide in someone and she liked him, even though she hardly knew him. Some producers handled the correspondents like stars, children to be stroked and humored, then gossiped about, but she trusted him not to tell anyone. She told him the news.

She flew home July 10, and went to her doctor's office. He scheduled a sonogram for the following day, and that night she bled heavily. The next day, the specialist examined her and told her it looked like she was carrying twins, but it was difficult to tell because they were only six weeks old. One might be a blood clot rather than a fetus. In any case, he could find only one faint heartbeat. She started to sob.

After the sonogram she wrote in her calendar, "No sign of baby." One fetus was definitely dead. But the doctor recommended she hold off until the end of the month to conduct another sonogram because of the confusion over whether the other was a twin or a clot. Either way, it was almost certain the baby or babies were dead.

July was the slowest month at *60 Minutes*, with the show in reruns. Nearly everyone went on vacation, and Meredith and Richard retreated to a weekend house they had bought in upstate New York, where she brooded about the bad news. This baby had represented so much: a belief that her earlier fertility problems were over because Ben's birth had erased them; a different way of life; a return to happiness. She now saw that in the recesses of her mind she had counted on the baby as a way out, a temporary escape hatch from a situation that never seemed to improve. It certainly wasn't why she was trying to get pregnant, nor had she thought about what she would do beyond her maternity leave, but once she had learned she was pregnant she had thought, "All I have to do is get through nine months and I'm gone again." For a while, she blamed herself because she had been on an airplane.

She was unhappy. Even trivial events seemed to be becoming a test of wills. Cashin, for example, had recently called in a panic to report that someone from *60 Minutes* had told her that they were about to move Meredith's office to the main corridor, next to Hewitt's office. Cashin, who was also on vacation, managed to delay the move until they returned from vacation, but Meredith suspected this was a power play.

She planned to keep the miscarriage a secret from Don, and she confided her intentions to a producer. What was there to gain from divulging it? she asked. If Don finds out from someone else—and Meredith already had told someone she hardly knew—all hell would break loose, the producer warned, urging Meredith to reconsider.

• • •

When she told Hewitt, he replied, "Does this mean you want to have more children?" "Sure," she said, affecting confidence. Hewitt rarely hid his emotions, and Meredith could see him stiffening. He said nothing, but he did not need to say anything more. His churning was almost audible, and she left his office feeling chastened.

The details of her pregnancy plans she would keep to herself, but she was not going to stop trying. Children were not some unmentionable disease. Meredith told others about the miscarriage, and word spread quickly through the office. Holly Fine wondered how Meredith was going to manage with a second child, given how protective and controlling she was with just Ben. She told Meredith she needed to learn to lean on more people to help her and that she had to develop good relationships with people who could help her at home. This would free her to work more comfortably. "You've got to give something up," Holly told her in one of their many conversations. "You've got to go one way or the other."

Cashin was also surprised that Meredith had become pregnant again so quickly. "Here's the best job in the world and she's going to have another baby?" she thought to herself. "How are we going to do this?" But she was determined to help. When Meredith saw that her new office left no place for Cashin except in a small area occupied by the water cooler and plants, directly in Hewitt's line of vision, Meredith offered to share her space, "You can move into my office." That was Meredith at her best, trying to ensure Cashin did not feel uncomfortable, when Meredith knew she was the one in the real line of fire. "This is silly," Cashin demurred, gratefully.

• • •

Meredith's doctor told her the fetuses had died because her hormone levels had dropped and recommended that she refrain from flying for a few months if she conceived again. Though her doctor did not believe altitude changes affected the uterus, other doctors did, and he thought it made sense to eliminate every possible risk. That meant flying only during the two weeks of every month following her menstrual period but before she ovulated again.

One by one she pulled her producers aside, confiding her plans and soliciting their help. She assured them she was not looking to reduce her travel, just to confine it. They were working on stories that required her presence in Spain, Los Angeles, Switzerland, Michigan, Connecticut, and Massachusetts—and she would go during that window. But she also told them that once she became pregnant she would not be able to fly for about three months. She knew she was beginning to become a liability to her producers, who were expected to have stories on the air, and she wanted to give them an out. They needed to be able to protect themselves if they thought they could not work with her request.

"I am not going to tell Don, but you are always going to be the first to know," she told one producer, asking for confidence.

The restrictions would be tough. It wasn't always easy to arrange interviews, and if Meredith got delayed with another story, forcing her to cancel an interview, several weeks might pass before the interview could be rescheduled. But all said they could manage. For all the logistical problems, most of Meredith's producers wanted to make it work. She was kind and easy to work with, unlike some of the other correspondents, who could be temperamental. Her first trip during her August window would be to Barcelona, Spain, for the José Carreras story. In the meantime, she would have plenty of writing and reporting to do in the two-week periods when she would not fly. Not all travel had to be eliminated—passage by train or car would not affect her, and she had several trips scheduled to Washington. She was still putting the finishing touches on the piece about the San Francisco nurses treating AIDS patients—which would probably run in the fall—and she had interviews scheduled in Washington for a story about the influence of Japanese lobbyists.

In late August, she traveled to Washington to screen an initial cut of the AIDs piece, "Ward 5-A", with the Fines. At its conclusion, she stood up and hugged the Fines. "This is incredible," she told them, tears streaming down her face.

Meredith took the script home with her to rework it, staying up late into the night. When she returned it, the Fines were impressed at her speed and her improvements. Like the best *60 Minutes* correspondents, Meredith really knew how to write, they thought. They told her it was wonderful, buoying her spirits.

But back at the office Meredith was feeling tense all the time. Hewitt was still complaining about her appearance—he questioned her decision to wear jeans in the AIDS segments and told her she needed to get a better haircut—and she was convinced he had moved her to the office near his to monitor her. She hated it. With the one wall that fronted the wide-open work area where everyone congregated made of glass, she felt completely exposed and on display. To maintain her privacy, she closed the blinds of her office on that wall, but that only heightened suspicions and hostility in an environment where all the others kept their blinds open, and strode in and out of each other's offices without announcement.

"What's she doing in there, nursing that baby?" Cashin overheard someone say one day. She and Stone were now engaged in an almost nonstop conversation about what they could do to make it easier for Meredith. "Tomorrow instead of closing the blinds let's keep them open, so they can see what we're doing," suggested Cashin, who was beginning to feel like a trained monkey, reacting reflexively.

The tension worsened when Meredith brought Ben into the office September 6 because her baby-sitter had a problem. "Don Hewitt goes berserk," Cashin wrote in her calendar that day after Don loudly asked her what Ben was doing there.

Despite the pressure and the anxiety, Meredith was determined to make it work, and when Hewitt chose her story about the black actor Charles Dutton for the season premiere in mid-September she hoped it was a promising sign. The season premiere was always a big deal among the correspondents, and Hewitt had passed over a lot of other pieces to choose hers, saying he loved it. After his lukewarm responses to her first-season stories, maybe this meant he was coming around. (His surprisingly blunt assessment to one magazine interviewer had been that he'd grade her stories for the last season a B or a B+. The generally accepted norm at *60 Minutes* was an A.)

Feeling a little more secure, Meredith left the following day on another four-day trip. It was the start of her window for travel. She also had a four-day trip planned to Geneva, Switzerland, as well as a day of work in Washington and a three-day round of interviews in Philadelphia, Rhode Island, Connecticut, and Massachusetts.

Just as she was wondering if she could keep up the pace, her AIDS piece aired on October 20 to wide acclaim. Hewitt was wild about it and critics cheered it. "The Fines and correspondent Meredith Vieira treat the victims with a dignity that society has conspired to deny them," wrote Tom Shales, *The Washington Post*'s TV critic. "The camera seems to be invisible, and Vieira shows how she earned and deserved the patients' trust. . . . 'Ward 5-A' is clear, direct, clean—no spurious heart-tugging, no melodramatics."

Any security she began to feel quickly started to unravel in early November when she was told that Harry Reasoner planned to retire at the end of the season. Reasoner's departure was always Hewitt's real deadline for her return to full-time status, and full-time travel. To make it worse, Meredith was told she had to fire one of her producers to make room for one of Harry's. She was given three names from which she could choose to fire.

"I'm not firing them," she told Don, confronting him in his office. These were people who had been loyal to her and worked extremely hard under difficult conditions. She accused Don of acting in bad faith. She reminded him that when he was trying to hire her he had promised she could pick her own people. But now, once she had picked some, he decided he didn't like them. It

was a slap in the face. "You're a liar," she yelled unchar-
acteristically. He told her she had no other choice, and
stormed out of the office. "I am not going to do your
dirty work," she said, trembling.

The next day Hewitt told her that Eric Ober, Burke's
replacement as the president of CBS News, wanted to
see her. Hewitt had complained about her outburst.

"Good," she said, getting up from her desk to go to
Ober's office. Ober listened to her complaints but told
her she had to do what Hewitt wanted. She interpreted
Ober's remarks as "Don is the money man and Don will
win." It was unusual for Meredith to confront Hewitt
and when she considered the episode in retrospect she
thought it was odd that it didn't involve her job directly.
It was as if she had been able to vent her frustrations
only through someone else.

Anguished at having to make a decision, she notified
each of the three producers and asked Cashin to pull all
their records: the production schedules, the research, the
stories that aired, the stories that fell through. There was
no way she was going to get rid of St. Pierre, who Hewitt
thought took too long to finish pieces. Meredith thought
she was superb. So it was down to Stone—the only person of the group that she had brought in indepen-
dently—and another producer. Hewitt and a number of
the senior people had made it clear from the beginning
that they did not like Stone, and Meredith assumed they
thought she would fire Stone. But she thought their complaints were unfair, and she pored over the material. Up
all night with her stomach churning, she finally made a
decision. The other producer was slicker, but Stone was
the better reporter. The next morning she told the other
producer she had decided to let him go.

"They already have a thing about you, and you have to know that," she added, after explaining how bad she felt. Sooner or later they were going to do him in.

The male producer left her office and exploded. Meredith listened as he ranted: all Meredith wanted to do was get pregnant, she'd told him a million times she didn't care about the show. Meredith felt terrible.

Cashin made notations on four days in her calendar that week: "Hell week. Don Hewitt goes nuts"; "Hell week"; "It's a bad day"; "It's a bad day." This was turning out to be the worst working situation Cashin could imagine.

Hoping for an escape from the tension, Meredith and Richard attended a dinner party at a close friend's home that Saturday night. Midway through the party, Meredith mentioned to another woman, a fixture in Democratic party politics, that she wanted to have more children. She suspected, but did not know for certain, that she already was three weeks pregnant. "But I'm a little nervous about what that means with the job," she said. Even reporting only half the stories she could barely cope, she said.

The woman looked startled. "You can't fail," she admonished.

"Why?" Meredith asked.

"Because all these women are now watching you," she said.

These were words Meredith did not want to hear, even though she had used similar ones about being a role model in interviews. The words sounded hollow now.

Richard, who was nearby, listened wearily to the conversation. Pressure took all kinds of form, he thought, with peer pressure among the worst. Meredith was already on a collision course. If she continued down the road this woman suggested, perpetuating the myth of having it all, that meant all the component parts of her life were going to be given short shrift. She was doing the best work of her career in his opinion, but it was killing her. The pressure was making her crazy and taking its toll at home. The little time she was not in the office she might as well have been. He was frustrated with her and angry at Hewitt. They had been foolish to believe Hewitt would be flexible and laid-back. It was as if Don Hewitt lived with them 24 hours a day. His scream, recounted by her staff—"Where is Meredith? Where is Meredith?"—echoed in her ears when she was home. She was always tense. Every time she went on a trip, she left the house crying. "You can walk away from this," he had told her one day as the tears streamed down her face. "You can just leave." But he knew it wasn't that simple for Meredith. *60 Minutes* was still the brass ring.

The following night, Meredith's piece about the efforts of a Michigan prosecutor to jail drug-abusing pregnant women, "Kim Hardy May Go to Prison," was broadcast.

Meredith's doctor confirmed she was pregnant. Now she would not travel by plane at all until she was out of the danger period—probably not for another three months. She told her producers they had to find stories on the Eastern Seaboard that she could reach by train or car.

Jane Stone was in Los Angeles working on a story when Meredith called. Stone had arranged a series of interviews there for Meredith which she had just rescheduled for the third time, having canceled two earlier times when Meredith could not make it. "I'm sorry," Meredith said. "Oh, no," Stone replied. The story would have to be put on hold indefinitely because Meredith was not going to travel across the country by train. "We have to do something," said Stone, fully aware of her own fragile status. She had not had a story on the air for some time, and once she returned to the office, she started combing through her files for possible story ideas. She found an old newspaper clipping from *The Washington Post* about an abortion clinic where women had been seriously injured. One woman was paralyzed, another had died.

Meredith normally turned down story ideas pitched by her producers, including Stone's, because she was always in search of only A-plus stories. She and Jane even had a long-standing joke about it:

"Meredith," Jane said, "I have a good story. It's the Second Coming. We have an exclusive."

"It's already been written," Meredith responded, her voice dropping. "In the Bible."

This time there was little hesitation. Meredith was in trouble, and this would buy some time. They both needed to show they were shooting and busy. Suzanne St. Pierre told Meredith her travel restrictions would not interfere with Suzanne's current story, which was set in Washington, D.C., and Pennsylvania, both reachable by train or car.

Meredith asked St. Pierre what she thought about her plan not to tell Don. That was a decision she had to make on her own, St. Pierre said, but she did not think Meredith needed to tell Hewitt in the first three months, given her history of miscarriages. "At some point you must be very upfront about it," she counseled. "If word gets around and you haven't told him that would be disastrous."

In the next three weeks, Meredith traveled four times to Washington, D.C., three times to Philadelphia, and once each to Baltimore, Maryland; Columbus, Ohio; and Albany, New York.

After one of her Philadelphia trips, a producer she had inherited from Harry Reasoner pulled St. Pierre aside. He and Meredith had gone to Philadelphia for a story about an antidrug crusader named Herman Wrice. The weather was freezing cold, and she and the crew marched through a Philadelphia neighborhood along with Wrice on one of his demonstrations.

"You know she is a great interviewer," he said, St. Pierre later recalled. "The only person I can remember going out with who was that good is Mike."

Before the end of the year, two more of her stories ran: "The Coach," about a high school football coach who was the object of complaints from parents about emotional and physical abuse; and her José Carreras story. She hated the Carreras piece when she saw it. She thought it was obvious that she hadn't been connecting, that her mind was elsewhere. Don told her he loved it.

In early January, Meredith picked up the phone at her home. It was Don, calling from London. "I've got a great story for you," he said, almost panting. "Catch the next Concorde to Paris." It was Saturday night.

Meredith's heart raced. She was still not out of the

danger period for flying, but maybe she should say yes. It would be easier than telling him. She stopped herself. "Don, we have a problem."

He said nothing.

"I did not want to tell you this way and I am sorry, but I'm pregnant and I'm not out of the woods yet."

An elongated pause followed. "I have to get off the phone to call Morley," Don snapped icily.

Meredith hung up the phone, trembling. I almost traded in my pregnancy, she thought.

At home that night she told Richard that Don knew. Even though Reasoner was retiring, she had decided to ask Don for another year's extension of her part-time agreement.

"Meredith," Richard said plaintively, "if you get it, that's what's called a Pyrrhic victory. We still have to live with the crazy man."

She next told Cashin that she planned to ask for an extension. "I'm doing this," she said with determination. She wanted one last chance to see if she could make it work. At some point soon, Ben and her new child would be in school, and then everything would work out. She had three stories nearly ready to broadcast: an investigation of employment practices at a chain store; an examination of charges that unsafe blood had been distributed by the Red Cross; and her profile of the antidrug crusader.

Maybe it can work, Cashin thought. She could see Meredith was not to be dissuaded.

Meredith had put off telling her mother, remembering how chilly she had been when Meredith announced her first pregnancy. But Meredith thought the time had come to tell her, and maybe this time she might react with excitement as she had with her brothers' children. "What's going to happen to your job?" her mother asked. Meredith sensed from her tone that she was disturbed. Meredith could feel her anger rising, but she knew fighting would only make her feel worse. Her mother obviously thought she was making a mistake. Having a big job was more important than having another baby. Would her mother like her less without television? Meredith cut the conversation short and hung up, her confusion about her choices amplified by her mother's implicit disapproval. Would she like herself less?

When Hewitt returned, Meredith could tell he was avoiding her. She had a lot of work to do on the abortion-clinic story, including several days of interviews in Washington, D.C., which temporarily kept her mind elsewhere. But the tension of not discussing the pregnancy with Hewitt was spilling over at home. When their dog Willie was hit by a car and seriously injured, she erupted at Richard, chiding him for not being more responsible.

Don finally approached her. He wanted her to fly to Russia. "It's a sensational story," he said. "The Ural Sea has dried up because of all the toxic waste that was poured into it, and there are now fishing boats stranded 20 miles from where water used to be." Al Gore, then a senator, was interested in the story, and he might go along. He asked Meredith to check into it.

Meredith had just moved out of the danger period for

flying, but there was no way she was going to a toxic-waste site pregnant. She was afraid to ascribe her reluctance to her own fears, however, and she called Gore to explain her worries. She wanted him to say she should not do it.

"He said he would not advise anyone who is pregnant to do it," she reported to Don. "I'm really sorry I can't."

Don said little in response. Unable to bear the anxiety any longer, she later entered his office. They needed to talk, she said.

Her baby was due in August, and she intended to take the six months permitted under the company's policy for maternity leave, she told him. "That brings us to February," she said. "I won't be able to get 20 pieces done by the end of the season. I don't want to lie to you. I can start cranking them out now, but I won't be able to do that much." She wanted to work one more season part time.

Hewitt seemed surprisingly calm. Maybe they could work it out, he said, because Lesley Stahl wanted to work part time. "Let me think about it. Let's see if we can't make it work," he said.

This was the first Meredith had heard that Stahl might be coming to *60 Minutes.* Tough and relentless, Stahl was one of the iron maidens of television. She had a daughter and a husband, but that was not her primary identity. When had Don begun talking to her? In July when she told him about the miscarriage? She was too relieved to worry about that.

Hewitt asked when she planned to stop having children. Reading the question as a friendly one, she laughed. "I might be kidding myself. I might want another in a year," she said, letting down her guard without thinking about the self-destructive consequences of her candor. A one-year extension might not be enough, she added.

Meredith left the office feeling great. She tended to hedge her bets, as she often did in tight squeezes, and she felt she had pulled through on this one, without thinking about the consequences. "You know this doesn't solve your problems," Richard said when she told him. "You can barely cope with one child. How are you going to handle two?"

Hewitt left the meeting uneasily. Though he had said he might be able to work it out, he realized he had made a mistake. He was being too soft on Meredith. By February the other correspondents were dragging and complaining about the traveling in general. The complaints ran through his head: "Holy Jesus." "How much longer do we have to do this?" "You're going to kill us." "I can't go on the road again. I haven't seen my family. I haven't been home." Safer recalled a year when he was home only six weekends. Hewitt could only imagine what they would say if he told them they were going to have to work harder to keep the show afloat while Meredith was having a baby. Wallace, in particular, would be furious. He'd complained to Hewitt that Meredith wasn't carrying her weight, and even had called Lesley Stahl in July to ask her if she was interested in coming aboard, because Meredith wasn't working out. Wallace couldn't figure Meredith out at all. All kinds of people would love her job; an orangutan would want it, he thought. For his dough, Wallace had said, she wasn't cutting it.

Hewitt, who prided himself on his instinct, was ticked off at himself for not seeing this from the beginning. He should have realized that hiring a woman whose primary interest was in having babies would mean that eventually everyone would have to work harder. Had he been smarter, had he probed a little deeper, he thought, he would have asked her during their negotiations what would happen after her two years of part time were up. How are you going to feel about it? Hewitt consulted with a few people at the office and decided he couldn't agree to another part-time deal. He called Eric Ober, who called Meredith the next day. "You either have to work full time or not. We can't have part time," he said. She interrupted. Hewitt had told her she could split the time with Lesley Stahl.

"Don didn't really mean that," he said.

Meredith called her attorney, Bob Barnett. There had to be a way to work it out, she insisted, ignoring that she already had trapped herself once into promising more than she could give. All she could see was that the career she had spent 15 years building was slipping away.

The following evening, Meredith and Barnett met with Ober and two of his top deputies. Don was absent. CBS would still honor her contract for two more years on another show, she was told, but it was all or nothing with *60 Minutes.* The reality pained her. No one was playing the heavy, but it was clear that this time there were no more detours, no more jury-rigged options. It had to be nothing. How could she be away from home for 100 days a year with a new baby and a small child? Working a little over a year and part time, she'd already been on nearly 50 trips and away from home nearly 75 days. Why have children if she was not going to be with them? But first she wanted one small concession: her replacement would be full time. Hiring a part timer would suggest her performance had been lacking, she calculated. They agreed.

As the meeting came to a close, someone from CBS suggested making an announcement that Meredith had chosen to leave the show because she wanted to take care of her children. Meredith balked. "I won't go along with that," she said. She did not want it to sound as if she just wanted to have babies—because she did not. There was an issue here.

Within hours word that Meredith was leaving the show had leaked, and pointed queries were being made. Most reporters interpreted it as a firing, and no correspondent had ever been forced to leave *60 Minutes*. That the first one to go was pregnant was fast becoming big news. Questions about sexism at *60 Minutes* were surfacing, and Don was on the defensive.

"My decision had nothing to do with the pregnancy," he said in one of a series of interviews he gave that day. "The people who work on this program have the roughest job in TV journalism; we need people who can turn out stories. We don't have bureaus. Our correspondents are physically traveling the world. They're exhausted; the workload can't be spread around."

To back up his claim that gender had nothing to do with his decision, he said 11 out of 25 producers on the show were women, more than any other news program on TV. "This is not a man/woman issue. It's a journalism one."

Though still in a state of shock, Meredith remained calm and direct. "I felt I was a contributor and that part of my appeal to viewers was being a working mother," she said, "working stiff, if you will, as opposed to a star. I'm sorry to lose the job. I wish they could have shown some flexibility, but I understand. I felt like I was a trail-blazer; there are a lot of women coming up through the ranks, and if you're working towards the top jobs, it's almost as if you can't raise a family too. . . . I'm 37 now and I was looking forward to a long career with *60 Minutes.*"

Meredith could see that the network was trying to blunt any suggestion that her case reflected the network's hostility to pregnant staffers in prominent jobs. That day she was asked if she believed she was a victim of sexism.

"I don't want to stand on a soapbox and say that women are getting screwed today," she told a *Newsday* reporter. "I'm not convinced that happened here, although there are people who are convinced that it did. But I wouldn't agree that this has nothing to do with sexism."

She added: "My baby is more important than Don's baby, and my feeling was, 'Yes, you can love both,' or at least I thought you could." *Newsday* followed up with a scathing editorial: "Sacking pregnant employees is no longer the thing to do. . . . Dropping her from the show is a throwback. The *60 Minutes* clock must be running backwards."

When Meredith read the follow-up stories she knew there would be trouble. Though she had told most reporters she might have made the same decision had she been in Hewitt's place, those words were missing from the stories, and Hewitt was almost manic about criticism.

Hewitt was fuming. He was not a feminist, he was not a masculinist, he was not a sexist, he was not a racist, he was not an ist of any kind, he said. He'd always been attracted to strong career women. He pointed out to whoever inquired that his ex-wife, Frankie, ran the Ford's

Theater in Washington, and his current wife, Marilyn
Berger, a current *New York Times* reporter, was a writer.
Why was Meredith being treated like the hurt party
when the fact of life was that her devotion to her baby
conflicted with her ability to do her job?

Cashin noted in her calendar: "More press—Don
pissed off." Meredith wrote in hers: "Don flipped out
about suggesting he was sexist." She also recorded the
results from a recent test checking the health of the fetus:
"Amnio result came back. Everything is okay." The good
news gave her perspective, but it was muted by Hewitt's
counterattack in an interview with *The New York Times*,
that appeared March 4. "For reasons I don't understand,
she never made anybody sit up and take notice," he said.
"Your fingertips tell you that nobody was talking about
Meredith Vieira." In another interview he went further.
"Look, in a nutshell, if Meredith Vieira had created half
as much attention working with us as she's created complaining about us, I would have turned handsprings to
keep her here," he was quoted as saying, adding it was
wrong to suggest as some had that Meredith's problems
were the result of not fitting into a male-dominated
show. "She brought her baby! I set up a nursery so she
could nurse her baby in the office. You know who was
horrified at that? The women around here who had had
their babies and gone back to work. They couldn't believe it." He added that her appearance was of concern.
"Her coming in in blue jeans never bothered me. It bothered everyone else. One of the girls said, 'For Christ's
sake, the cleaning women come in here looking better
than that.' I said, 'This woman is worth waiting for to become one of us.' And then one day, she said, 'I can't be-

come one of you.' What have I been waiting for all these years? Why did I set up a nursery?"

Meredith felt sick. She had brought Ben in while she was still on maternity leave, but he had come with her only a handful of times since she had officially started and then only in emergencies. There was never a crib and there was hardly a nursery. He might feel now that having a baby interfered with her ability to do the job, but it was unfair to suggest that she had misled him about wanting to participate in her family's life. She felt she had been direct. But it was the criticism of her work that hurt the most. She had worked hard. She was not a prima donna. It seemed to her that Hewitt was trying to derail the criticism of him by attacking her, not an atypical tactic, and his comments were casting a huge shadow over her career. She called Eric Ober.

"I'm not going to stand by while my career is being destroyed," she said, almost shouting, her fury masking her sense of failure. "It's Don's show, but it's also my reputation."

Next, she called Don. "No one thought your work was that good," he told her.

"You're a direct guy. You say what you think. You never said that to me," she responded. "None of the other correspondents said that to me."

Don backed down slightly, agreeing that maybe he should not have been quite so blunt. But he countered, "You never seemed committed to the show."

He was right up to a point—she knew she was not committed in the same way everyone else was, but that didn't mean she wasn't doing her job. She hung up the phone. She and Don had never been on the same wavelength. It was foolish to pretend otherwise. He had said more to her about her Carreras piece than he ever did about her AIDS story.

The damage, however, was done and Meredith, who was assigned to the show until May, forced herself to go into the office. Hewitt wasn't talking to her—communicating only through news articles and memos—and others were pointedly ignoring her. They clearly blamed her for dredging *60 Minutes* through the mud. The media was using the incident as an opportunity to examine *60 Minutes* under an unflattering spotlight; chauvinism was a common theme. In a story in *Rolling Stone* magazine Wallace acknowledged that he had snapped women staffers' bras.

Other colleagues, like Holly Fine, treated her with sympathy. Even though she thought Hewitt's decision was ultimately a fair one, given the workload of the other correspondents, Fine wished Hewitt had held on longer and given Meredith more time to get her life in order. Meredith was an exquisite writer, easy to work with and not temperamental or egotistical. She was a decent person and had a great ability to bring out the best side of people in interviews. Meredith needed to learn to organize her home life better and not sweat so many of the small things, but Holly wondered if Hewitt realized what a talent he had lost.

Small gestures of kindness touched Meredith. Morley Safer stopped her in the hall one day and asked her what she was going to do next. She said she did not know. To this day, he told her, his daughter and his wife were disturbed that he had been gone so much. She felt he was telling her she had made the right decision. Anthony, the Chicago boy she had featured in her *West 57th* story, called her shortly, assuring her she was doing the right thing. "Nothing matters more," he said, his words providing a momentary relief from her self-doubt.

Meredith asked if she could return to Romania to report a follow-up story about selling babies for adoption; she was out of the danger period of her pregnancy and it was a way to escape from the office tension. She was told the story was being held for the next season. But a week later Meredith noted that Lesley Stahl was on her way to Romania for *60 Minutes.* The next week Stahl arrived to spend a day in the offices. Meredith felt that she was being punished for being pregnant.

At the same time, news articles continued, stoking Hewitt's temper, and the strained truce erupted again near the end of March, when *The New York Times* ran another article, a highly critical column that said Hewitt had been accused of insensitivity to women's issues in the past. The story suggested that Hewitt had an added responsibility to show more flexibility because of the high visibility of television. "I think it's in the best interest to bend a little if you have a talented person," the story quoted one CBS executive. "Meredith is a talented person. The bottom line is it could have been arranged."

Hewitt was enraged, believing that Meredith now had crossed the line and was feeding a vendetta, even though the story said she had declined to comment. He could not believe Meredith's case was becoming a cause célèbre, the vehicle for debating attitudes toward working mothers. He was tired of being painted as the ogre and was relieved and encouraging when women staffers drafted a letter saying they had never experienced sexism on *60 Minutes.*

"Surely Meredith knew what an extraordinary concession Don Hewitt was making for her by sanctioning her flex-time work schedule for her first two seasons," a draft of the letter read. "She was expected to do 10 stories a year. In the first year she managed only five. The fact that she is pregnant again is terrific. But fair is fair. *60 Minutes* needs a full-time correspondent now—one who can drop everything at a moment's notice to pursue a great story. That is how we remained in the top 10. It's not sexist. It's practical working journalism."

Suzanne St. Pierre was sitting at her desk in Washington when she received a call from one of the women writing the letter. She was told a dozen women had already signed. "First of all, I am not going to sign it," she said. Second, she said, "It is a very bad idea."

In hindsight, St. Pierre thought *60 Minutes* had probably come along at the wrong time in Meredith's life. She had so much else new on her plate, and to succeed at *60 Minutes*, a correspondent had to have everything in her life organized. But it was hard to second-guess Meredith's decision to take the job. The offer might not have come around again. Meredith was a good, decent person with a lot of talent, particularly as an interviewer. Other correspondents often relied on the producer to supply the questions; with Meredith it was a real conversation. There was room for improvement, but there had been with every new correspondent. She hadn't been surprised that Hewitt had lashed out. He'd also criticized Diane Sawyer's work publicly when she left, but the letter was cruel and unnecessary.

Meredith, who had been told about the letter, was furious and hurt.

Others balked at signing, too, and a contingent suggested to Hewitt that maybe sending the letter was not a good idea. It was too painful for Meredith. Hewitt agreed, but he was upset and through Cashin sent Meredith a memo that was conciliatory, in part:

> I have always believed and I will continue to believe that the *only thing* that makes any difference at *60 MINUTES* is how each of us performs his or her job.
>
> Some of the women at *60 MINUTES*, who were reluctant to join in protesting a *N.Y. Times* column that said that isn't so, apparently also feel "that isn't so." I don't really care *who*, but I sure would like to know *why*.
>
> It serves no purpose to pretend that all of this isn't tied to some of what is real and some of what is perceived about my feelings towards you. What is real is: You are a superb reporter and a superb mother who, not entirely of your own doing (I'll take the rap for a lot of it) ended up in the wrong kind of work at this time in your life. You are quite right to say "My baby is more important than Don's baby."
>
> However, out there in broadcasting are several "babies" just waiting for you—jobs that will give you the attention you more than deserve from the public, and your children the attention they more than deserve from you.

Barely a month later, St. Pierre was fired from *60 Minutes,* less than a year after she had signed a four-year contract.

• • •

From time to time Meredith fantasized about quitting, but Richard was still freelancing. If she quit, they would lose her income and her health insurance, and one of her major worries was always Richard's illness, with its uncertain course.

Richard had never been as concerned about their income as Meredith, and he told her he was more worried about her loss of confidence. He had not thought it was unreasonable for Don to turn down her request to continue part time, but he believed the criticism of her work was unconscionably mean. It was unhealthy for her to remain at CBS. "Once your reputation is tarnished it's almost impossible to rebuild it in the same framework because such a case is built against you," he said, recalling his own experience.

"You can find work," he said. "I can find work. What's the big deal?" They lived relatively modestly. Their house in Westchester was large, but not fancy, and not completely furnished. They had one car, a battered Volvo station wagon, that matched a lot of their possessions. But Meredith tended to expect the worst in these situations, imagining that her children might starve or that they'd be out on the street. Meredith felt she owed it to her family to make a decent salary while she still could, and the company had said it would continue to pay her the same salary. Who knew how much longer her marketability would last and who else would pay her that kind of money now? Television placed a premium on youth and good looks, particularly for women, and there was a window of time during which she could earn a lot of money. *People* magazine had just selected her for their annual edition of "The 50 Most Beautiful People in the World"—but she was nearing the cut-off age.

By the end of the season Meredith had exceeded her quota of ten stories but she had almost no work to do. When her second-to-last story aired on April 21 she was reminded of how much she was giving up. In "Suzanne Logan's Story," she described the unwillingess of abortion-rights groups to alert the public to dangerous abortion clinics out of fear that any negative publicity would harm the movement, despite the obvious health hazards. "As a reporter, I found that many pro-choice leaders knew about problems at Hillview, but didn't want them publicized," Meredith said of one clinic where women had suffered botched abortions that led to brain damage, a hysterectomy, and even a death. A representative of the National Abortion Federation acknowledged it was aware of the problems. "Well, I think your first reaction from us was this is the last thing we need," the spokeswoman said during the broadcast. "We had hoped that it wouldn't get national publicity because of the political nature of this." The story was a classic *60 Minutes* piece. It exposed hypocrisy; skewered a liberal sacred cow; warned off other women from going to the clinic, and strongly suggested a remedy—legislation. It was an A+. But Meredith was feeling useless. Shooting for the next season had started, and Lesley Stahl was firmly in place. Meredith called network officials and asked if there was anything she could do. "You're paying me," she said. They assigned her a story for the prime-time show *48 Hours,* and one for a new courtroom show called *Verdict.* She winced when she heard the promotions for the pieces, announcing her debut. It sounded like a tabloid.

On her final day at *60 Minutes,* she braced herself as she walked into the studio, wearing a yellow maternity dress that was too bright. She was scheduled to film a new introduction for her "Ward 5-A" piece, which was scheduled to appear as a rerun during the summer. She had been packing up her office, and she could not help feeling as if she were reluctantly putting an important part of her self in storage. She had no idea what she was going to do.

Cashin had submitted her resignation for May 31 and couldn't wait to leave, but she could see that nothing hurt Meredith more than having to leave *60 Minutes*. Meredith was the ultimate overachiever. Failure was not in her experience or her vocabulary.

On August 2, 1991, Meredith gave birth to Gabriel Anthony Cohen, choosing his middle name in honor of the Chicago boy she had featured in her *West 57th* story on hunger. Meredith began keeping a scrapbook, a gingham-covered photo album with a quilted cloth bear on the front. She was afraid that when her child grew older he might feel his birth was a bad thing because of the controversy. On one page she pasted a photograph of herself, obviously pregnant, at a reception following a speech she delivered at Tufts in June. "Dear Gabe," she wrote at the bottom of a letter from a Tufts official thanking her for coming. "This was one of the first places where I spoke about giving up *60 Minutes* because of the baby in my tummy. . . . That baby in my tummy . . . that baby was you. I've never regretted the decision to place my family over my job. I love you, Mom." If she gathered enough mementos, perhaps she could convince him—and herself—that she believed she had made the right decision.

She was still shell-shocked. Everything had unraveled so quickly, and badly. Other producers outside CBS had approached her almost immediately about offers. She had listened, but considered none of them seriously because they struck her as schlocky. Friends suggested she try a morning show. She knew they meant it nicely: "You're a mother. You can move to the morning show." But she usually responded: "I'm a mother and I'm not good in the morning." She was not good at happy talk, the staple of those shows, and the subject fare was not serious.

She also did not want to leave CBS, however rough the ride had been. Her whole career had been there, and for a long time she had been treated like a queen. She wanted to prove she could succeed there again. Now that she had two young children, the idea of starting someplace new also was less than appealing. But as the months passed, Meredith kept putting off a decision. She knew it was now her responsibility to come up with some ideas. If she wanted flexibility, what did she propose? That was a harder question to answer. When a producer friend suggested she report for "Eye on America," a segment of the evening news, she realized how out of it she really was, as if she did not exist. She had no idea what he was talking about. She was normally busy bathing Ben when the news came on and didn't watch.

Near the end of her maternity leave, Meredith met with network officials to discuss her return. Someone proposed she could join the new magazine show *Street Stories.* Her former colleague from *60 Minutes* Ed Bradley was the anchor. Ordinary Americans, not celebrities, would be the focus. It was an appealing concept.

"Would there be a lot of travel?" Meredith asked.

"Of course, several days a week," one official responded.

"Remember all those articles that were written about me last year when I left *60 Minutes?*" she asked. Were they insensitive or trying to send her a message: "Get live-in help. You've done your mother thing. Get back to work." Or, she thought, maybe they thought she was like all the others: she would do anything to be on the air.

She would have been interested in the job at another time in her life, but she had learned her lesson from *60 Minutes.* She wanted to mother her children, and she could not do that the way she wanted and travel. "I would be setting myself up for failure. What's the point?" she asked a friend. But she was leaving herself with almost no options.

Meredith returned to work in the first week of February without a clear idea of what she was going to do. CBS officials came to her with another proposal—anchoring the early-morning news. The current female anchor wanted to move to the *Evening News.* She did not rule out the morning show, but her first reaction was that she would not do it. She was a reporter, not a newsreader.

At home that night, she reconsidered. Maybe it made sense, she told Richard. What did he think? She could be a real mom and still get a hefty salary. She'd read interviews with Katie Couric and Jane Pauley, the current and former anchors of the *Today* show, and they seemed to feel a morning show was ideal for a woman with small children. Their shows, however, started an hour and a half later. Meredith would have to be at the studio by 4:30 to prepare for the 5:30 taping, but she would be home by 7:30 or 8 A.M., in time to feed Gabe and Ben and then spend the day with them. With a full day ahead of her, she'd finally be able to do things for herself like see friends, read or exercise. She also had the option to report pieces for "Eye on America"—she'd since watched some tapes—which might satisfy her desire not to give up reporting completely. She also acknowledged that she hadn't actually come up with a realistic proposal—she wasn't a Maria Shriver or a Connie Chung who could write her own ticket.

Because Richard had just signed up with CNN's political unit to cover the 1992 presidential campaign, he would be traveling, and it was even more important that she be at home. He agreed with her assessment, and was pleasantly surprised that CBS had met her more than halfway.

But before she made up her mind, Richard urged Meredith to take a hard look at all the practical implications of the new job. "When is this going to leave any time for you or us?" he asked.

She said they could have dinner together in New York on the days she returned for the evening-news pieces and some nights they would even spend the night in the city.

She talked it over with a close producer friend, who encouraged her to take the job. It was a good compromise, she said, and it was doable. The producer thought it was a waste of talent, but Meredith wanted to be home.

"I'll take this job, but I don't want to go anywhere that I can't get back from the same day," Meredith told CBS officials. CBS and Meredith agreed they would reevaluate the arrangement in six months.

Even though it wasn't her first choice, she felt she had landed on her feet. She had to accept that she did not get her first choices anymore. She thought she could handle the downgrading, at least for a while.

Several months later on a warm Saturday, Meredith drove to the train station to pick up Richard and Ben. Trains were Ben's passion, and this was his reward for a visit to the doctor. There was an obvious tension between the two as they slid into the car, and Meredith suspected they had had another fight, as they often did these days. Richard said nothing during the ride home, and when he began walking silently across the lawn Meredith asked, "Richard, what's wrong?" Catching up to him, she saw the tears streaming down his face. A torrent of words followed.

At the Manhattan station he and Ben had jumped onto their train, holding hands, when Ben pointed out Richard's CNN identity card lying on the platform near the open train door. Richard leapt to the platform, and while he was bending over to recover the card, he heard Ben saying he was coming to help. Instinctively, Richard shot up his hand to keep Ben, he thought, in the train. Instead, he must have knocked him down into the gap between the about-to-depart train and the platform. All he could think of was keeping the doors open. Trains don't move when the doors are open, and he pleaded with passengers not to let the doors close. Then he remembered the third rail, the track that could electrocute Ben. He screamed at Ben not to move, and peering in the darkness saw his small figure near the train wheel. Put your hands in the air, he yelled, and when two little fists appeared Richard scooped him up.

"Look, you did the right thing," said Meredith, having recovered from the shock. She could see he was beating himself up, reliving the scene over and over again, as if he might have killed Ben. "He's okay because you thought."

Later, Meredith wondered what she would have done had she been in a similar situation. She didn't blame Richard, as she knew he thought she might, or attribute it to his illness, as she might have in the past. In fact, she realized that Richard was exactly the right person to have along if you were going to be in a bad situation. He was far more calm and logical in crises than she was. He would know what to do. She would not have known to keep the doors open.

Does anyone ever get accustomed to these hours, I asked myself as I walked down the halls of CBS News in New York at 5 A.M. one morning in December 1992, nearly nine months after Meredith had signed on as an anchor, and three months after the train incident. I had arranged to meet Meredith before the show's 5:30 taping. She had been up since 3 A.M., at the studio since 4:30. How did she make it? I wondered. "In theory, it's great," she had said on the phone the day before. "In reality, it sucks."

What a change, I thought, for a woman who just three years ago had vaulted to the top of television journalism. I had met with and spoken to Meredith several times since she left *60 Minutes*, but this was the first time I had joined her on a set.

She laughed at my obvious fatigue and pointed to the coffee when I slipped into the makeup room, where a stylist was curling the ends of her shoulder-length light brown hair. The pancake makeup failed to hide the exhaustion that creased her face. Meredith was pregnant again—seven months with her third child—and her belly protruded prominently beyond her pale gray jacket. She had not been trying to conceive and the pregnancy had been unexpected. Still, she touched her stomach and laughed. "I'll do anything to get off the show."

Ten minutes later, Meredith and I headed down the long, narrow corridor leading to the studio. Along the way, we passed poster-sized photographs of the network's stars: Dan Rather and Connie Chung, *CBS Morning News* anchors Paula Zahn and Harry Smith; Lesley Stahl surrounded by the men of *60 Minutes.* I had not known we were headed for Studio 44, the site less than six hours earlier of a 70th birthday gala I had attended for Don Hewitt. Meredith had not been included in Don's toast, a salute to the *60 Minutes* family, past and present. She was mentioned only once, and then derisively, in a rap song called "Don's Blondes," written and sung by Lesley Stahl and Diane Sawyer, her successor and predecessor, who took to the stage in long blond wigs. Spoofing Don's fondness for women correspondents with a certain glamorous look, the pair warned, "Let your roots go and you'll be out like Meredith Vieira." The crowd had laughed wildly.

The studio this morning was cold and nearly empty. Where men in tuxedos and women in gowns had stood, eating hors d'oeuvres served on silver trays, young men in T-shirts sat eating oatmeal from plastic-foam bowls.

Near the far end of the studio, where the musicians had played, two sound technicians slept in chairs. Meredith joked that the florid chiffon scarf around her neck had to stay, however askew, to cover up some baby spit.

Meredith flipped through the pages set on the studio desk making only one minor editorial change to the script—something about a children's entertainer—before the news director signaled her to start.

An hour later Meredith and I were headed to her house. With the Hudson River receding, I told Meredith I had been at the party. She looked pained. "It still hurts," she said, looking away. "It's as if I didn't exist."

Half an hour after leaving Manhattan, Meredith and I pulled into her driveway. It was 7:30 A.M. and the day was just beginning to lighten. Though close to Manhattan, Irvington felt a thousand miles away. Trees arched over expansive lawns and lanes; the golf course across the street from her house was covered in snow. Did I imagine sleigh bells? Meredith opened the front door. An excited shriek sounded from upstairs, followed by a clattering of footsteps. Within moments, Ben, nearly four and with hair so blond it looked almost white, appeared at the bottom of the broad wooden staircase, with the dog thumping his tail deliriously. Gabe arrived next from the kitchen, waddling unsteadily and trailed by Richard, a bowl of cereal in his hands. Both children were dressed—even if Ben's T-shirt was inside out.

Smiling and laughing, Meredith dropped to her knees, encircling Ben and Gabe with hugs and kisses.

After a quick cup of coffee and a rundown of the day's plans, Richard left for Manhattan. With Hanukkah beginning at the end of the week and Christmas ten days away, Meredith had delegated some of the shopping to him. We had an hour and a half before Ben's school began and Meredith suggested we moved to the playroom, a brightly lit spot half a flight up from the kitchen. We could talk there until her nanny arrived.

I had said I wanted her to evaluate her decision to leave *60 Minutes* for the *Morning News*, now that enough time had passed. Had she made the right decision? "On the one hand I don't feel the guilt about not being there for my kids. On the other hand I'm so tense all the time I don't know if this is the best thing for them," she said, balancing a farm toy in the palm of her hand.

"I want to be more relaxed than this. This isn't natural. There is no flow here. It's all very cut and dried, and I don't want that kind of household. On the other hand, if I had to be traveling all the time, I think I would have been so depressed not to be with them and not really be a family that that would have been miserable.

"I'm at such a loss now. I have no idea what the right answer is because this isn't it. But the old way wasn't it, either."

Part of it was physical. She'd had an ideal when she took the morning job—she would feel a sense of balance once she had more time at home. But she had failed to consider just how much a night person she was. She tried to go to bed by 7, but despite months and months of trying to adjust her internal clock, she still woke with a painful start when the alarm rang out at three and then, unable to face rising, bargained with herself for another half an hour. Her remaining sleep was fitful, and she had to drive herself out of bed just before a car arrived at four—without one it was doubtful she'd make it to the studio by four-thirty. By the time she returned home at seven-thirty she craved sleep, but she almost never took a nap. Mom time had started.

"No matter how long I do this shift I never, ever, get used to it. I'm always exhausted," she said.

She felt strung out, but she tried to hide it, usually bundling the two children up for an excursion before the start of Ben's school at 9:15. They had gone bobsledding the day before. After dropping him off for a couple of hours, she tried to decompress and breathe—read the papers, use the bathroom, and catch up on some work— if Gabe took a nap. Then, depending on the day, she took Ben to a gymnastics class or Gabe to a play class—to spend time separately with each. On Tuesdays a little girl came to play with Gabe.

"It's not because I'm some hero or martyr. It's because I feel guilty," she explained.

She had envisioned using the afternoons that she did not return to the office to work at home on "Eye on America" pieces, but she had found it impossible to work while her children were awake, even with a full-time nanny to keep them busy. She had tried shooing them out of the upstairs room where she worked on the computer, but she immediately chided herself for getting too caught up in her work, especially if she had snapped at them. Her standards for mothering were almost unattainable—a good mother should be always available.

"I say to myself, 'What am I talking about? I'll find

time in some other ways to do what I have to do. Right now he needs me,' " she said. But even when she interrupted her work to play with them, she always felt that she was falling short of her ideal—that she never gave them enough attention, love, support, or just giggles.

To compensate, she forced herself to rise two hours earlier, at 1 A.M., on days she had an "Eye on America" script due. One of her first assignments was a report about Americans' diminishing leisure time.

Richard had urged her to set boundaries, pointing out that what was good for her would be good for the children, and part of that meant freedom from children. They were happy and well-adjusted. They never interrupted him on the computer because they knew he would not tolerate it. "They play you like a violin," he said. He had started putting Gabe to bed at night because if Meredith did she would be in there for an hour.

As she talked, I remembered Meredith's telling me in one of our first conversations that the best time she ever had working was in Chicago for the *Evening News*. Why? I had asked. She answered promptly, almost without stopping. She was living by herself and had no responsibilities to anyone but herself. There were no competing forces vying for her attention.

She recently had informed her producers that she could not do any more "Eye on America" stories. She was too exhausted, and anyway they weren't satisfying. Field producers did most of the reporting, leaving her to write the script and narrate it. It wasn't exactly demanding intellectual work. But even after cutting this out, she said, their life still seemed unbearably regimented, because she was always rushing to get to sleep. Neither she nor Richard had foreseen how physically grueling the schedule would be.

"When 5 o'clock comes to this house it's impossible. 'Oh God, we have to feed the kids because we have to bathe the kids, because we have to read to the kids and play with the kids because we have to be in bed by 7 P.M. It sucks. It's like the military. I don't think life should be like that. There is nothing relaxed about our lives."

With so much focus on the children, she left almost no time for herself or Richard. Since they were too tired to keep their promise to stay overnight in Manhattan on days she worked downtown on "Eye on America" pieces and too tired when they were home, intimacy between them—emotional and physical—had all but disappeared. They took turns reading Ben bedtime stories, and one was usually asleep by the time the other came slipping under the covers. To keep on the same schedule, Richard rose shortly after Meredith. He was as tired as she was and she worried that the fatigue would set off his neurological problems, as it had in the past, though she refused to confide in anyone at CBS about this. She thought it would be used against him.

"We're just wiped out all the time, and that's such a dangerous thing," she said. "What are we doing it for? What's the point? So we can pay one more mortgage bill, but there's no family anymore? If the relationships are forced and there is a stilted quality, it's regimented in a way that isn't natural. I don't want to make it into more than it is, either, but there's always this underlying tension."

There was no downtime. "I'm not trying to sound like some prima donna, but I think you have to carve out time solely for yourself. Two of the biggest regrets I have about this job is that we have no more time as a couple and I certainly have no time as an individual. I almost resent it if Richard works out in the morning. I feel like 'Why don't I get the chance to?' But then even if I had the opportunity, I'm so tired I can't take advantage of it. So it's tension when I come home."

Friendships had always been important to Meredith, but those too had gone by the wayside except on weekends, when Meredith insisted on returning to a regular schedule to have some normalcy in their lives. They might have dinner then with friends, but come Monday they paid for the extravagance in additional fatigue.

"There are people who are on this shift and think this is the best thing in the world." As she spoke, her voice was becoming more rapid. "I thought I could manage it. Is it just that I'm never going to be happy? I have an image of juggling things because I don't want half things."

Meredith realized she had adjusted the external circumstances of her life somewhat, but the problems were more complex—or at least different—from what she had initially assumed. Internally, she had not let herself off the hook. Even with help, her standards for mothering were inflexibly high—an almost impossible ideal of warmness and availability—and she'd also been unable to relax her own high professional expectations. She had thought she could downpedal professionally for a while and be content as a competent anchor, or a newsreader as she called it, but she had not.

She cringed when interviewers suggested her career had taken a major tailspin, and she hated it when colleagues complimented her on being such a good mother.

114

"Even if I chose that and wanted to be that, I can't stand it when they say it. They've made the separation: You're not a professional, but you're a really good mom." The good thing about the hours was that she had only run into someone from *60 Minutes* once, the commentator Andy Rooney, on the way to his office early one morning.

But it was Meredith above all who felt as if she had failed, not just everyone else. Even though she had clearly made the decisions to leave *60 Minutes* and anchor the morning show, she couldn't live with the consequences because she had not considered how important her work was to her sense of self.

"I don't do anything anymore," she said. She did not write the script or gather the news. She just read what was on the teleprompter and went home. "It's not what I do best or what I got into the business to do," she said. "So it's very frustrating . . . they could pay you a million bucks but it wouldn't matter."

I had spoken to Don Hewitt in the course of my interviews with Meredith, and he had posed a question that I now wanted to repeat to her. We had moved to the kitchen table. Hewitt had told me that he had reacted badly in criticizing her work and that he regretted it, although he continued to believe he had made a sound professional decision—not a sexist one—in not allowing her to continue part time. He said he had seen her across the room at a going-away party for a colleague shortly after she started the morning news job and that he wondered how she felt being a newsreader. "Where it may accommodate her life, her family life, I can't believe it can be very soul-satisfying to someone who seems to have a natural curiosity to learn about all the things that good reporters want to know," he said to me, suggesting some identity with Meredith.

I repeated his question to Meredith. He had called it the $64,000 question: "Now let's assume that ten years from now the kids are in school and they're doing fine and she's ready. Will anybody want her then? She's got to think about that. I only hope, my fondest hope is that she never ever says to one of those kids, 'Do you know what I gave up for you?' I would hope that she never says that. I would like to believe she never will. But she would not be the first one who did."

Meredith paused, a painful look crossing her face. "It's not at all satisfying. It can't be. My training is as a correspondent, so this will never be satisfying where it might be for someone else," she said. But she added, "I will never ever blame my children."

She started to cry and her voice began to break. "I'm just tired. I love my kids so much. I blame myself sometimes that I just can't seem to do this. For some reason I just can't seem to find the measure that works."

She knew it was going to be even harder to manage with a third child, but she at least had made up her mind to leave the show in February when her child was born. Even though the pregnancy was unplanned, she was happy and relieved. She wanted more children, and a new baby would provide an excuse for returning some normalcy to their lives by getting off the morning show.

There remained the question of what she was going to do with her career. She had to work; Richard's work with CNN had ended with the election, and he was looking into other jobs. She had hired an agent to explore other possibilities. Executives at ABC and NBC had expressed an interest, as did those in public broadcasting. But she knew that with three children she might be on her last legs professionally. Who was going to want her? One high-ranking official at a competing network had told her he would love to have her work for them and assured her that they could be flexible; they had been with other working mothers. But after about half an hour he acknowledged that maybe he was making it sound better than it actually was. "He said, 'I've got to tell you when you get behind closed doors, even here, it's the same old thing. It's that they just are not interested in women who have kids and women who won't commit fully'."

Phyllis McGrady, an executive producer at ABC, had approached Meredith at an awards dinner to tell her she was very interested in having Meredith come to work on a new magazine show. McGrady had said she understood Meredith's concerns about traveling and she said she would be willing to accommodate them.

Meredith had been intrigued. She knew now that she had underestimated how vital her work was to her sense of self and had made too big a swing from *60 Minutes* to the morning job. She had mistakenly thought she would be able to bury her own needs in her children for a while, and that would be satisfying. Instead she had had relatively limited and unimaginative choices thrust upon her because she hadn't really made any decisions about what she wanted in her life. This time she planned to proceed differently, and to travel some.

"Maybe I could have let go a little bit on one end or the other," she said. "Maybe I'm setting goals for myself that are too difficult in wanting to be perfect. The perfect mother, the perfect journalist, the perfect employee, the perfect wife. And what you end up getting when you set all these goals is imperfection on every level."

Richard thought it was a journey without end. There were no good solutions. But it was critical to get their lives back.

On February 7, 1993, Lily Max Cohen was born. Shortly after Lily's birth, a producer who was also a friend visited and asked Meredith if she wanted to join the staff of Connie Chung's new show. She asked how much traveling it would entail.

Two weeks out of every month, he said.

"Why would I leave the top-rated news-magazine show to do the same amount of travel on an untested product?" she asked. "There is no way I'm going to do that."

He was a close friend, but he said he couldn't make any exceptions. Until then Meredith had not been ready to break the emotional link with CBS, despite the feelers from other networks. Now she knew she had no other choice, but the conversation reminded her of how much she still thought about not having made it at *60 Minutes.* She'd recently spent some time with the mother of one of Ben's classmates, who'd quit a large Wall Street firm, where she was a high-level executive, because the company was unwilling to accommodate her request for flexibility. The woman told Meredith she was bitter and felt she would have to leave her field and do something entirely different, because otherwise she would feel she was being punished for becoming pregnant. She did not want to be second best in her field. Meredith worried that she was still bitter, too. Let go of it, she counseled herself.

In late spring, she entered into serious negotiations with ABC and NBC. Andy Lack, her old executive producer at *West 57th* who had been so understanding and accommodating to her desire to have a family, had been named the president of NBC News, and he wanted her to work for *Dateline,* their magazine show. She could work part-time, but she would also be paid only by the piece. He was sweet and she had fond and grateful memories of how well he had treated her when she was pregnant. Still, she did not think she could afford to take the financial risk of such an arrangement.

That left ABC. Roone Arledge and others were pressing her to join their new show, which would focus on one subject for an hour each week. Before making any decision, Meredith laid out all her concerns. She wanted flexible hours and limited travel. She wanted to be able to work out of her home without fear of jeopardizing her position. If they couldn't live with her requirements, or she couldn't do what they wanted, it was better to know up front and not enter into an agreement she could not keep or they would not be comfortable honoring. No glossing over this time.

ABC executives, in a series of meetings, assured her they understood what her problems had been at *60 Minutes* and that they wanted to be as flexible as possible. They wanted her to travel five days a month, but it did not matter where she worked or when as long as the work was completed. There were no objections to putting the terms in writing in her contract. They were willing to pay her about $400,000 a year.

The pitch appealed to Meredith. She liked the idea that all the top producers were women, and sensed that their gender made them more sympathetic to her family concerns and more sincere in their guarantees about working at home. Although she worried about what kind of stories and packaging they might have to use to secure ratings to keep a new show on the air, the one-hour documentary format appealed to her. She could be vigilant about making sure her stories met her standards. She was still anxious about traveling, but Richard, who was working on a project for public television, told her if she did not care about the income he would take off six months and work at home on a novel he wanted to write. That meant he would be home, available almost all the time. Both their needs could be met. Meredith thought it was worth trying. She was willing to make more trade-offs now than she had been in the past and delegate more family responsibilities, having experienced the consequences of limiting her options the last time and of trying to keep too tight a hold over the household. She hadn't always been fair to Richard in the past, when it came to caring for the kids, and his quick thinking in the train incident had probably saved Ben's life.

In August, at the end of her maternity leave, Meredith informed CBS she would not be returning. She was scheduled to begin work at ABC in early October.

She was anxious, but she felt she finally had found people who seemed to understand her need to balance her life. "We get it," was a refrain repeated many times during her negotiations. She had come to believe it. More importantly, Meredith had started to learn the elements of a balanced life and the need for her to take primary responsibility for creating it.

Still, she had no illusions she had found the perfect solution. "As long as I hold down a job I am going to struggle with this question: Will I be a good enough mother?" she said. "But this job at least allows me an opportunity to try to be the mother I want to be and to stretch myself." No more Pollyanna. But far fewer tears.

Rachael's STORY

Rachael Worby, the conductor of the Wheeling Symphony, punched in the phone number of the governor's mansion in Charleston, West Virginia, furious with herself for having agreed to dine, alone, with Governor Gaston Caperton. She already had postponed her arrival by an hour and now planned to delay for another. How much longer could she stall? It was one thing to accept his invitation to join the state university board, as she had done after they met at her annual symphony ball in the winter. But this, she knew, was not business. The 50-year-old governor had separated recently from his wife of 23 years and had since become increasingly persistent and personal in his overtures.

Rachael had seen enough local newspaper stories linking the governor to other women to underscore her impression that he was another tall southern playboy who dated celebrity women. Besides, she viewed politicians with a suspicion just short of contempt. The closest she usually came to one was to pose with her arm around a cardboard cutout as a joke. If he expected to add her to his list of sexual conquests, she told herself, he could think again.

At 8 P.M., Rachael finally arrived, three hours late. She was wearing her usual uniform of all black—an oversized jacket and pants, with three earrings piercing her right ear. Though she was 40, her tiny 5'2", 100-pound frame, waist-length dark brown hair, and large, attentive eyes gave her the appearance of a hip and artsy gamine, who also was drop-dead beautiful. She crossed the portico into the mansion and quickly surveyed the ground floor. She was an intelligent woman, who could be generous and warm, but she could also be a perfectionist, who quickly passed judgment on any effort that failed to meet her high standards. In her eyes, someone's home revealed his or her personality in the same manner a diary disclosed longings, or physical appearance an image of elf. The rooms of the mansion, traditional and formal, looked just as she had imagined—predictably safe. "I'm not going to like this guy," she murmured to herself.

An assistant told her the governor was waiting for her in his private quarters on the second floor, a request that momentarily unnerved her. She had expected to eat in the large public dining room—in an open space.

Gaston leaped to greet her. At 6'3", he was a lean man with a handsome angular face. He was wearing jeans, with an open-necked shirt and loafers without socks. In a soft southern drawl, he teased that he had been waiting since five. Rachael's mind was elsewhere. The door had opened into a series of rooms as tastefully understated as the public rooms had been overly grand. A brightly colored wooden replica of a Noah's Ark caught her eye first; how bold, she thought, to place it next to a massive Chagall-like canvas—and just right. Her eyes next moved to the contemporary art work lining the other walls: a poignant photo essay on coal miners; a Miró; an etching. Flowers, including some of her favorites, were everywhere. Books—art, history, architecture—were stacked on the tables, and an overstuffed white sofa anchored the room, offset by chairs with a lively geometric pattern. A fire was lit in the fireplace and opera played. This was her native New York—stylish, confident—not West Virginia. Gaston poured her a glass of wine.

She pulled herself up short. "I can only stay for half an hour," she said, announcing she had a meeting at 8:45 P.M.—an escape route she had planned in advance. When an assistant entered to announce dinner, she pounced. Did he always have someone say: "Dinner is served?" she asked in what she tried to make seem like a joking manner. But her words landed with the directness of a frontal assault. Dinner was brief. After taking a few bites of salad at the candlelit dining-room table made of glass, Rachael pushed backed her chair. She really had to go, she said. Gaston said he would like to see her again. Did nothing faze him?

"If we see each other again we will get in trouble," she answered, surprised that she was being charmed despite her best intentions.

"When's your birthday?" he asked. "I'm taking you to Paris for your birthday." She laughed and left.

Pulling out of the driveway, Rachael slumped. She had appeared confident and defiant in front of the governor, but that was bravado. Alone, she felt confused and beset with self-doubt. She was one of a handful of women in the country to lead her own orchestra, but the achievement had come at a cost. Her husband of three years, a screenwriter and producer named David Obst, had recently asked her for a divorce. He was fed up with all the time she spent in West Virginia and New York (where she also was the music director and conductor of Carnegie Hall's Concerts for Young People), away from him and their home in Los Angeles. He had backed off after she asked him to reconsider—she'd even offered to quit her job in Wheeling—but the marriage seemed to be headed inexorably toward a brink, the victim of too many errors to count.

Three years earlier, when she was 37, she had impulsively accepted his marriage proposal a few weeks after they met—the same month she auditioned for the Wheeling job—for what appeared to be all the wrong reasons. David had professed immense admiration and need for her, and she was usually attracted to men who made her feel she could help them. Besides, her parents had adored him, and their approval always counted a lot—too much—and she felt it was time that she married. All her friends had. Now, she dreaded returning to Los Angeles where they had lived like nomads since selling their small house, encamping in progressively smaller and dingier motel rooms with kitchenettes, constantly in search of a less expensive place to stay because they had been unable to find another house they wanted that they could afford. At his urging, she had given up the one place she loved: a cheap, rent-controlled apartment that she kept in New York.

These days, she wanted to leave Wheeling, too. Three

years after taking over the symphony at a salary of $25,000 a year, she felt like the Michelin boy, trapped in a too tight tire, pressing into the walls of the symphony and the town. Rachael had left her job as an assistant conductor for youth concerts with the Los Angeles Philharmonic, one of the top symphonies in the country, to take over the Wheeling Symphony Orchestra, at the bottom of the totem pole, because she needed to have her own orchestra to develop as a conductor. In Los Angeles she would always be an understudy, limited to the concerts no one wanted to play—holiday programs or performances for kids. Besides, Wheeling was the only symphony to make her an offer out of the many before whom she had auditioned. The symphony had improved markedly since her arrival; she no longer had to order some members to "ghost bow," without touching the strings, because they could barely play, or worry whether a player's hearing aid might start ringing loudly during a performance, as it used to do.

Still, West Virginia was hardly a center of sophisticated cultural life. Even though her own upbringing had been lower-middle class, art and culture had been important in the family's tiny house in the Manhattan suburb of Nyack, New York (Rachael described the house as two-and-a-half bedrooms because her room was a converted sleeping alcove). Outings to Broadway or the Radio City Music Hall were common, and there was always $5 for her weekly piano lessons, even when her father earned a modest salary from a variety of sales jobs, including selling used cars and peddling encyclopedias door to door. He played Gershwin and Cole Porter nightly on the piano while her mother, who had perfect pitch, could distinguish a misplayed F for an F-sharp from the kitchen. But in the Wheeling auditorium where she conducted, the country-western radio station, Jamboree USA, received top billing on the marquee, while symphony announcements were barely visible on a small blackboard. She had auditioned with bigger orchestras in the past two years, but had yet to make it beyond the finals.

As she recalled her dinner with the governor, she knew it was irrational to find him more attractive because his sensibilities appealed to her or that he had an impressive art and music collection. But without much of a husband or a home, and worried about her career, she was vulnerable. She needed to stay away from him.

But within days the governor started calling. He followed up with appearances at her concerts and postconcert receptions. He popped over to her favorite restaurant in Wheeling, Ye Olde Alpha, which had a publike feeling, and he stayed late, talking, as if he had nothing more pressing to do. When he invited her to a large dinner at the mansion, she accepted, but asked a male friend to escort her. She found herself seated at the governor's table, her escort at the most distant one.

Gaston was a gentle and effusive man by nature, prone to praise in most of his daily interactions. With Rachael, he turned the spigot on full force. Her insights were brilliant, he told her. "You are so far beyond this orchestra," he said another time after a concert, telling her exactly what she wanted to hear. Rachael was more urbane and culturally sophisticated than the governor. She had earned an undergraduate degree in piano performance from the Crane School of Music at the State University of New York. Later she had attended graduate school at Indiana University and then studied for her doctorate in musicology at Brandeis University (though she had never submitted a dissertation). She read voraciously and punctuated her conversations with literary references. Had she had higher self-esteem, she might have dismissed Gaston's outpouring of compliments as the expected gush of the uninformed, or accepted them simply as a kind gesture or part of an obvious seduction ritual. But Rachael had grown up feeling she did not come up to scratch, a secret fear she still harbored, and she always used admiration from others to prop her up.

Still, she wondered, could he be real? He certainly did not fit her type. Most other men in her life had been talented, troubled individuals in need of rescue. With them, she had been able to play savior and in the process feel, at least temporarily, better about herself. If she fixed their problems, they might love her. But Gaston seemed to be in better shape. Though he was in political trouble for breaking his campaign promise not to raise taxes, he acted like a grown-up, someone who could handle his own crises. Why would he want her? What role would she play? He was aristocratic, calm, and religious. In his basic interactions, he appeared to be kind, fair, and non-judgmental. He seemed a genuine optimist. She was the first to label herself as neurotic and temperamental, judgmental, controlling, a perfectionist.

Gaston persisted. He invited her again to the mansion and sent a car to Wheeling, two and a half hours away, to pick her up. Sitting in the backseat, she panicked. What were they going to discuss? On other occasions she had tried sparring with him, but he would not engage in it; she could see that her well-honed verbal artillery devastated him. She had no experience of a peaceable discussion with a romantic interest. She asked the driver to pull the car over to the side of the road while she considered canceling. Finally, she told the driver to continue, reminding herself she had a hotel room as protection. She was not going to sleep with him.

After spending Thanksgiving with David, she secretly agreed to accompany Gaston on a three-day trip to Big Sur, California, where she insisted on separate rooms and registered under an assumed name at the Ventana Inn, an exclusive resort overlooking the Pacific Ocean. She made similar demands during a secret trip to New York, where they stayed at the intimate Box Tree Hotel. She had not made love with him and still would not. Her head was spinning with anxiety, but she could not let him see this. In front of him, she acted independent and strong, tough and defiant—a model of the liberated woman she wanted to be. This was her armor. Enjoy yourself, she told him, live the single life. He had no obligations to her, as she had none to him.

Over Christmas, he took her advice and arranged a skiing trip to Colorado without her. When she could not reach him one night by phone, she left a message. As the night progressed without a return call, she phoned again. Still no answer. "Call regardless of time of return," she said this time. The next morning she woke abruptly to the telephone ringing. It was Gaston. He had not called the night before, he said, because he had met a friend, a woman television broadcaster, and they had gone out and had a wonderful evening.

"I can never see you again," Rachael said, cutting off the conversation. The competition had suddenly brought her immense insecurity to the surface. Maybe she cared more than she thought and he less than she thought.

Gaston called again when he returned to West Virginia. She had always been so tough and resistant, he said, that her vulnerability was unexpected and caused him to search his soul for the remainder of his trip. He said he realized he could be one of the most eligible bachelors in America, dating other women, or just have Rachael. He wanted only her. He asked her to join him for New Year's Eve at a house lent to him by a friend.

"I cannot have sex with you," she said, shortly after arriving. "We've never talked about money, sex, or religion." Gaston laughed. "I have a lot of money, I want to have sex with you, and I'm an Episcopalian." On New Year's Day they made love for the first time.

Rachael had rarely engaged in casual sex. She liked to touch and hug her male friends, jump in their laps, and kiss them on the lips—flirtatious gestures that many thought meant she might be sexually available. But she had had only a few real sexual relationships before Gaston. Even then, she felt ambivalent about the physical act and tried to satisfy the man first, staving off intercourse and insisting reciprocation was unnecessary. Her reward was his pleasure.

She recognized that much of her discomfort with sex probably stemmed from her childhood. Her mother had never spoken to her about anything remotely connected to sex, not even menstruation, and seemed extremely uncomfortable with her own body. Rachael had never seen either of her parents naked, and she was still amazed by her mother's Houdini-like ability to change her clothes in the open-space dressing room at the women's discount clothing store Loehmann's without anyone's ever seeing her undressed. Rachael had inherited her mother's embarrassment and felt ashamed of

her body in front of men. She thought there was something unclean about it or that it was inadequate.

But it wasn't just her mother's discomfort with her
own body that affected Rachael's ability to enjoy sex. She
had spent much of adult life struggling in vain, she felt,
to gain her mother's approval, and she repeated this pattern in her relationships. If she pleased the man, he
would love her, and that was all that mattered. It was devotion and attention she craved, not pleasure. She had
not masturbated or had an orgasm until she was in her
30s. She had slept with her husband, David, only a handful of times.

Gaston was different. When she tried slipping into
bed wearing underpants, a T-shirt, socks, and a sweat-
shirt with a hood, he clicked on the light and gently told
her she could not come to bed like that. He loved her
body, she had beautiful breasts, he told her softly while
she cried. He wanted to please her.

A week after New Year's, Rachael called David, on his
birthday, and told him she now wanted a divorce. She
did not tell him about Gaston. Even though he had
wanted a divorce, knowing there was another man
would hurt him. As impulsively as she had decided to
marry David she now decided, secretly, she was going to
marry Gaston.

Sitting on the counter in her kitchen in Wheeling,
Rachael next called her mother in New York. She steeled
herself. Her mother, Diana Worby, was a bright woman,
who had enrolled in college for the first time after her
children were grown and later had gone on to earn a
doctorate in literature. She now taught literature at an
experimental college. She had always demanded a lot
from Rachael. "You are just going to have to explain this

to me," Diana said sharply, Rachael later recalled.

"I do not love David," Rachael responded.

"What in God's name does that have to do with anything?" she remembered her mother's shouting. "Do you think that's what a marriage is based on?" She and Rachael's father had talked about love a little bit in the first year of their marriage, she said, but never after that. Rachael could feel herself tightening. She thought her mother had always tried to control her life, and Rachael almost always reacted with defiance. She'd stopped playing the piano as an adolescent for a year in rebellion against her mother's demand that she practice nightly, only to resume secretly. Only then did she enjoy the piano for herself. And as a young adult she changed her childhood name of Susan to Rachael. She had never liked the name Susan, but the change was more than an aesthetic whim; it was also a way of breaking her parents' hold, making herself more independent. Her parents at first refused to call her Rachael, but she had not budged then and she was not going to budge now.

She hung up the phone, feeling she was replacing a defective relationship with a secure one, that maybe she had found a union in which she could combine love and work. Gaston, she believed, was the first person who was not on her payroll who seemed to believe in her as a conductor. When she was a child and told her parents she wanted to be a conductor they told her she should set her sights on being a music teacher; in contrast, she had heard her father tell one of her brothers he could be president of the United States. Her male conducting instructors were similarly discouraging, insisting she would fail because orchestras, dominated by males, would never respond to a woman. After so many naysayers, she was not going to give up the kind of support Gaston was offering.

That month she filed for a divorce in New York on the grounds of abandonment and asked for a speedy resolution because she planned to remarry. Obst agreed not to contest, and a few weeks later on February 23 the divorce was granted.

A few weeks after Rachael told David Obst she wanted a divorce, I picked up the phone at work and found Obst on the other end. He and Rachael had come to my wedding a few months earlier on November 25, 1989, and I told him how pleased we were that they had made it. I asked him to thank Rachael for the warm and sweet note she had just sent. "It's not working out," he said. Their marriage was over. He gave no other details, and I, silenced by the disclosure, asked for none.

I did not know Rachael or Obst well then, and I did not know anything about Gaston. Our husbands had had a friendship and professional relationship years earlier; my relationship with Rachael was like that of many people who assume the earlier associations of their mates. But the times I had met Rachael I liked her. She seemed almost incandescent with exuberance. She laughed uproariously at David's stories, her braid switching across her back like a whip. She played Elaine May to his Mike Nichols. She was one of those people of whom my mother would say, "She makes an effort." When I had mentioned casually at our first meeting that I had never seen an orchestral score for a symphony, for example, several pages appeared on my desk at my office the next day with an explanatory note.

After Obst's phone call, I looked at our wedding photographs and found several shots of Rachael beaming at David, including one of her kissing him tenderly. I then reread the card that had arrived with a postage stamp of the composer Toscanini: "Just a brief note to say that your wedding party was simply wonderful—your love for one another seemed to generate a warm embrace around us all—it was an honor to celebrate with you and lots of fun, too! Much love, R." I suspected David, a master storyteller with a flair for drama, was exaggerating about the end of their marriage—or that I had caught him on a bad day.

Four months later, a small news story appeared in *The Washington Post* announcing the marriage of the governor of West Virginia on May 25, 1990, to Rachael Worby.

When I began my research the following year, I called Rachael. I knew political wives paid a special price for their relationships, and none shelled out at a higher cost than first ladies, who were expected to hew the traditional line. Rachael had a career, but Washington, my home, was full of so-called new political spouses with professions—often lawyers and lobbyists—who routinely shed jobs and opportunities that cast any shadow on their husbands' ascent, grafting their ambitions to their husbands'.

Rachael, in contrast, had spent none of her life in the role of political adjunct, and her job was entirely distinct from politics. Music had been the central focus of her life since she began piano lessons at five, and her role models were Leonard Bernstein and Janis Joplin, people who lived their lives outside the lines, shaking their fists at the gods or wailing at the top of their lungs.

To compete as a woman in the male-dominated world of classical music required enormous drive. Rachael, who had barely broken through, stood poised at a critical juncture in her career when she married Gaston. I knew she was in the midst of transforming the Wheeling Symphony from a mediocre local orchestra that performed a handful of concerts a year to a strong regional one with nearly three dozen annual concerts. Her success there would determine her future.

Had she known what she was signing on for? Was she aware that she had taken on one of the most traditional of female roles in one of the most tradition-bound states? Her professional goals seemed destined to clash with the demands placed upon the wife of a politician. Could she resist the political and social demands that would draw her energies from her career? Would she be able to balance her need to support her husband with her own goals? Or would she live a split life? She told one audience: "I believe I represent the new West Virginia woman: one who's dedicated to the responsibilities of family and marriage but who also has the desire, and most importantly the freedom, to pursue her own career and her own dreams." Would it remain so?

My other questions were about her happiness, her daily life, and how she handled the conflicts. Could she make everything fit?

Over the next few years, I came to know Rachael well, and in the process to know Gaston also. In addition to my phone calls and trips to see her, the two came to Washington half a dozen times, usually on business. We dined together, and they were guests in my home. We traveled together twice. I quickly came to see Gaston's appeal. He enthusiastically embraced life. When excited, he would rub his hands together with joy, his fingers fully extended and the air bristling with the sound of flesh. He was relentlessly inquisitive about everything, unafraid of being called naïve if he did not know something. As a breed, politicians tend to be good talkers, but Gaston was also a good listener.

Together they were good company. Gaston had reserves of energy, and there was nothing remotely low-key about Rachael. She was in your face the moment she entered the room. A night with them meant an evening of good conversation, an adventure.

It was for these reasons that I was always struck during our interviews by the jarring disparity between her public appearance of effortlessness and the churning, psychologically complex pain she revealed privately. She spoke with frankness and candor, willingly laying bare the inner turmoil of her life. Her candor was unusual for any woman, but even more extraordinary given her public role. She was almost compulsive in her need to unmask her life. The reasons for her frankness were at first not apparent to me, but I later came to see that they lie at the heart of this story.

As the clock approached midnight on February 1, 1992, Rachael noticed that Gaston, who had been at her side in the receiving line at her annual symphony ball, had disappeared, looking grim, after a state trooper passed him a note. Concerned because he had not returned, Rachael slipped away to search for him. She found him downstairs on the phone. His rival, the state's attorney general, had just announced that he had changed his mind and planned to challenge Gaston for the Democratic nomination in the upcoming primary in May.

Rachael tightened. This was exactly what she had hoped would not happen. When she and Gaston had discussed whether he should run for reelection, she said she could handle a general election campaign, which would heat up for only about three months. But she could not imagine campaigning for nine months, from February to November. She had urged Gaston, who also didn't want a primary, to pull out all the stops to ensure there would be none. Each time a possible contender surfaced, Gaston and his allies stroked him, pulling him back into the fold. What had happened?

She had entered the ball that night convinced the tactic had paid off. The attorney general, Mario Palumbo, had taken himself out of contention a month earlier, when he announced he was not going to run, leaving only three others candidates, none considered serious challengers. The filing deadline was only hours away.

Rachael did not want to stand in Gaston's way—and she could see from his expression that Palumbo's entrance was a severe blow—but at that moment she could think only that her life was about to spin out of control. She and Gaston had been married a little over a year and a half and although she never admitted it publicly, the role of first lady had been a lot more stressful and demanding than she had imagined. Naïvely, she had expected her transition to politics to be smooth because she had lived her life on the public stage as a conductor. But traits she once considered her beauty marks soon had become warts. Columnists made snide personal remarks about her public displays of affection to her husband; sitting in his lap at a football game or nuzzling him appeared to be verboten.

Even her seemingly inoffensive efforts to cultivate the arts and reduce illiteracy came off as arrogance. Rachael had initiated a televised series of lectures on the arts at the mansion right away and created a foundation to raise money to fight illiteracy. She had thrown herself into their promotion, making more than 200 speeches and visiting more than 50 cities in the process, and she spoke regularly at schools, exhorting the students to fight ignorance and intolerance and to dream big. Yet in some quarters her highbrow sensibility came off as cultural snobbery, the patronizing manner of her native New York.

In one series of memorable flaps, she told a newspaper reporter that she did not read West Virginia newspapers, only *The New York Times*—a habit she said she had developed because she did not like to read reviews of her music. She then attempted to mend the damage of that remark, telling another interviewer: "I don't have a religion of not reading newspapers. I can't get *The New York Times* here on a daily basis. I have to read something."

Rachael realized she had made some mistakes in her early interviews but columnists would not let up in criticizing what they saw as her elitism. "If Ms. Worby sometimes sounded a bit like Miss February listing her turnoffs, she nonetheless gave us a peek into a world where everybody knows what Flaubert said to DeMaupassant and nobody clips grocery coupons, even when they're doubled . . ." wrote L. T. Anderson, a popular columnist for the *Charleston Daily Mail*. "So now we know. Ms. Worby isn't bored only by cocktail party dullards. She's bored by an entire state."

The criticism stung, and now as she stood by the telephone in her black evening gown at the Viennese Ball, she could imagine it worsening. She started to simmer. She was mad at the attorney general. She was furious with the giant nondescript group she referred to as "Gaston's people." She was angry with Gaston. This could have been avoided, she said. But her anger, as it almost always did, masked her worry and fear. What effect would the campaign have on a marriage as young as theirs?

Gaston, no doubt, would approach the campaign single-mindedly. That was how he worked in a crisis, she had come to learn. There would be many mornings when he rose before she woke and returned home after she fell asleep, she was certain. She did not know if she could bear the absences. As bad as the politics were, they shared an intimacy she never imagined possible and she felt she had become a better person because of him. He wasn't afraid to check her tone of voice when she lashed out if someone disappointed her—a bad habit that he reminded her of about once a week—but he seemed to do it without judging her, reminding her people wanted to like her. He was usually right. Even though she still had a temper, she now could at least hear the sarcasm in her voice when her anger took over. It gave her chills. He ironed out the chaos inside her.

He had also become her most ardent booster—and made it clear he realized how important her music was to her. Her music sounded richer for it, she was sure. When she talked about finding another job, he urged her to redouble her efforts. Don't worry about the location, he assured her. Whether it was Sacramento, California, or Hamburg, Germany, they would work it out. The last thing he said he wanted to do was take her from her music. She did not know if she was strong enough to navigate on her own, as she would have to do with him campaigning. She depended on him as a mirror to see not only who she was but who she wanted to be, and her sense of self had become almost inseparable from his support, making any disruption to the relationship threatening.

Their physical closeness was almost preternatural; when she cupped her body to his and he placed her hand on his head, she felt an indescribable serenity—part comfort, part security. He called it the "sleeping pill" because he instantly fell asleep in this position. She was still somewhat inhibited sexually with him because she was afraid of letting herself go, but she was making an effort to be more open to his desire to please her. Already they spent too little time together. She had never wanted an Ozzie and Harriet life, in which every weekday was the same, but their separations sometimes spanned ten days—too long. Her jobs were in Wheeling—a two-and-a-half-hour car trip from Charleston—and in New York. When they were together they were two public people with public lives, like two dancing bears; everyone expected them to perform.

Before anyone knew there was going to be a primary they had instituted a rule of one weekend day of complete rest with no events, but even then they honored it in practice only about half the time. On one recent Saturday morning, they had been lounging in bed, nude, catching up on each other's lives after several days apart. Just as Gaston bent down to kiss her the whir of a helicopter filled the backyard. The phone rang. "Ten minutes, governor," said the voice on the other end. Gaston jumped out of bed, apologizing. He had promised to attend a state university football game. Later, they both laughed when she teased him that on his deathbed he would wish for more time with her rather than more football games. Now, it seemed less of a joke.

Rachael had an unrelenting habit of seeing everything in extremes of the best or the worst. Sometimes, this labeling helped her to adjust by taking steps to prepare for change, but more often than not it led to unreasonable and unfair expectations, exacerbating her disappointments. When she fell asleep that night, she imagined the worst.

She worried how a sustained campaign might affect her career and her efforts to move on to a better job. With a busy primary race, she would have less time for studying if she campaigned as much as most political spouses did, and there would no doubt be more negative stories about her. She was in the process of applying for several jobs, and she had heard rumors that her past might be a target. Leonard Bernstein had been not only her professional role model but her guide for outrageous living, and like Bernstein she had had an appetite for life's extremes in her youth. One of her favorite sayings was "If you remembered the sixties you weren't there." She had lived with men and had relationships with people who had drug problems. She had experimented with drugs herself. She wasn't ashamed of her past. She just thought it would not go over well with a 90s symphony board.

Personality and charisma were as important for a conductor as talent when it came to being hired. She had improved as a musician since marrying Gaston, but she could not help noticing that guest-conducting requests had become scarcer. The rejections demolished her, and some days she closeted herself in her room, crying and wondering whether she should quit conducting because she seemed not to be getting anywhere. It would not help to have some board member read that she was a degenerate or a witch or, worse, think her primary job was as a wife and first lady, as her agent already had warned her some did.

Rachael was still recovering from a recent meeting with a world-renowned conductor she had wanted to see for months. She had been hoping that he would invite her to spend a couple of weeks watching him rehearse and introduce her to some of his colleagues. Instead, he seemed distracted. Packing boxes littered his office, and a stream of assistants ran in and out as they spoke. After a few moments, the conductor looked directly at Rachael as if he had just hit upon a wonderful idea, "What I really think is, why don't you have babies?" Rachael was unable to control her response. "What do you mean, 'Why don't I have babies?' I don't want babies. I want to conduct," she said. He mentioned a young foreign conductor who was pregnant. "The orchestra just loved it." Rachael was insulted by the comparison. The other woman held only a part-time position with a much smaller orchestra. She could not believe she had waited eight months to have a conversation with one of the top names in her profession and they were talking about babies. After 20 minutes, she handed the conductor a video of herself conducting and left, her composure barely intact. Inside the cab, her eyes flooded with tears. The conductor had seen her exactly as she struggled not to be viewed: a woman first, a conductor second.

The day after the symphony ball and the attorney general's announcement, Gaston left at dawn for a three-day governors' conference in Washington, D.C., before they had a chance to talk it out. The biggest concert of her life was coming up that Thursday—the flutist Jean-Pierre Rampal was performing with the symphony—so she remained behind in Wheeling for rehearsals. But even had he stayed, she knew, Gaston probably would have recoiled from an emotional discussion about the primary. He did not like confrontation and most likely already had picked up the pieces of his disappointment and immediately shifted into gear to do whatever needed to be done. She envied his ability to act swiftly and decisively, compartmentalizing the emotion from the work at hand. Boom. Click. High gear. She had seen it. Call Frank Greer, his media man. Call Geoff Garin, the pollster. Call the campaign manager. Move. Move. Move. He was an optimist, who always believed he could win if he tackled something hard enough. She, on the other hand, tended to replay her anxiety and rage and fear over and over again, like an old record with the needle stuck, unable to move unless someone tapped it with a finger, especially in relationships. She could feel herself digging deeper and deeper into a rut.

She had to pull herself up. She had never conducted anyone of Rampal's standing, and she needed to concentrate. She no longer worried that the orchestra would fail. Her efforts to hire better musicians, including talented young players from neighboring states, had paid off even if it was at the cost of severely alienating local players, who criticized her harshly and publicly. The orchestra now played the most difficult pieces with polish. Their performance of Shostakovich's Symphony No. 8, one of her favorites, was superb. She was determined that her biggest musical moment not be marred by a failure of concentration, but she could not help fretting, and as the hours passed her anxiety worsened.

Before Rampal's arrival and between rehearsals she called Gaston's campaign aides. She called members of his staff. "What does this mean about my life until May 12?" she pleaded. "Just tell me." She tried reaching Gaston, but with meetings from breakfast to midnight, he was almost incommunicado.

Rampal's arrival on Wednesday temporarily alleviated her anxiety. She had to speak French all day with him and entertain him during the off hours. She wanted to make sure everyone, from the board members to the audience, was satisfied. She was not disappointed. Rampal was a huge success and paid her the compliment of staying to listen to the orchestra perform Beethoven's Seventh Symphony after he had finished—an unusual gesture of admiration. She told friends later that he had said he loved her Beethoven, and that she must have French blood in her because the orchestra's performance of a Ravel piece, also part of the concert, was lush and impressionistic. For a few moments, Rachael swelled with pride.

After another concert the next day, Rachael returned to Charleston to meet with Gaston and his staff. They had mapped out the next three months and showed her the preliminary calendar. Once she saw something on paper she began to calm down. The process was finite—or so it seemed. Gaston had warned her that weekends were of

the essence in a campaign, so at first the addition of another barbecue did not surprise her. Then a pig roast was
penciled into the calendar. Every weekend—including
their one day of rest—was taken. Rachael urged restraint. "I need breaks," she pleaded, and so did Gaston.
But no one seemed to be listening. All noncampaign
trips outside the state were canceled, starting with a
long-planned trip the following weekend to New Hamp-
shire to see friends. A skiing trip was canceled to avoid
the barrage of criticism Gaston had endured at Christmas after he and Rachael had gone to Vail while the state
was in the midst of a major advertising blitz to sell West
Virginia as the Colorado of the East.

One of the first events on the schedule was a black-tie
dinner for the state legislators at the end of February. As
a state official, the attorney general had received an invitation. Rachael promptly told Gaston she would not
stand in the receiving line to greet him. "I will not dirty
my nest," she said. When he urged her to consider the
ramifications of such a snub, she said she would stand in
line and hand the attorney general a tape measure so he
would lose no time in taking the dimensions for new fur-
nishings. He winced. Rachael saw the world in terms of
friends and enemies. Everything was a personal attack.
She did not understand that in politics today's enemy
might be tomorrow's friend. She was still smoldering at
the refusal of Jay Rockefeller, the U.S. senator from West
Virginia and a former governor, to lend his name for an
early fundraiser, when every other federal politician in
the state had done so. Gaston could not afford to alienate
Rockefeller, regardless of his disappointment. Rachael
was more blunt. She told friends that "Jay is welcome in
our home, but not in our hearts."

Gaston urged Rachael to focus on her music and not the campaign. He told her he had already lost one marriage to an unhappy woman who accused him of holding her back, and he knew that Rachael was almost incapable of doing anything halfway. He did not want her to feel she had been put in a position similar to that of Sharon Rockefeller, Jay's wife, who curtailed her activities as the president of Washington's public broadcasting station when Jay was considering running for president. Sharon seemed angry, Gaston told Rachael, and he did not want to end up living with another angry woman. But Rachael was already on the verge.

They had their last relatively unencumbered period the weekend of Gaston's birthday, February 21. Rachael had invited a group of friends to meet them at an Italian restaurant in New York, but even then she and Gaston almost missed the dinner. A pair of murderers had escaped from a state prison and Gaston had turned back the state plane to deal with the growing crisis. They eventually arrived at their New York apartment only fifteen minutes before their dinner reservation. "Rachael thinks being governor is an inconvenience," Gaston joked when they finally arrived at Sistina, a brightly lit and busy Italian restaurant on Second Avenue. None of the guests worked in politics. Nearly all were Rachael's friends from the arts: including the actor Roy Scheider, the agent Sam Cohn, her publicist, a movie producer, and a cartoonist. When Scheider suggested everyone at the table describe how they had met Gaston, all except one said they knew him through Rachael. "When I heard Rachael had remarried I thought to myself, 'How do I get to see her without him?' because that was how I had always approached Rachael's attachments," one of the guests joked. "Now I wonder how can I see Gaston without Rachael?"

Later the next day, Rachael's eyes grew wide with dismay as Gaston described his campaign strategy. Sitting on a banquette in the dining room of the Mark Hotel in Manhattan, he explained that he had to figure out where his votes were and visit those counties five times. It had worked for him in his first campaign. "This is my worst nightmare," she said.

Gaston left for West Virginia and Rachael remained behind in New York. She had performances scheduled in several New York City public schools over the next two weeks. Even though they were only concerts for kids, and she had ambivalent feelings about playing five-minute excerpts of the great works, her weeks in New York energized her. She was, perhaps, the nation's best conductor of youth concerts, and children flocked to her as to a Pied Piper. She was like the favored, hip aunt who thrived on risky behavior. She skipped. She joked. She asked what they thought of pieces the orchestra played, encouraging them not to be afraid of classical music. "Listening to this will not require a lot of hard work," she assured the students at Public School 8 in Brooklyn Heights that week.

In New York she was Rachael Worby, conductor, not Rachael Worby, governor's wife. Her sleek, art-filled one-bedroom apartment overlooking Central Park afforded her an anonymity and culture-rich atmosphere that she could not find in West Virginia. New York was a sanctuary.

Yet the contrast also reminded her of the loneliness of her life in Charleston. Gaston was her only connection to life there. She felt she had no women friends. Some women she saw on a regular basis and she counted on them for companionship, but their lives and values, professional goals and self-conceptions, were utterly different from hers. Her tie to them was through Gaston. Her real friends—people with similar interests who had liked her before Gaston—were in New York, Boston, and Washington. Before they married, she hadn't really thought through what it would be like to live in Charleston, a place deep in the middle of the state, closer to Kentucky than to Wheeling, where getting even to New York required changing planes.

But having felt unloved for so long, she had been ready to be loved, and she had let the whirlwind of romance carry her away, obscuring the reality of how great a change this would be for her. Besides, Gaston's friends had embraced her, wooing her almost as much as he had, and assured her she would spend little time in Charleston because he loved to travel. He had taken her to Paris and Tuscany, and they spent many weekends outside of the state before the primary. But she had been naïve—or intentionally blind—to believe that as the wife of the governor she would not spend a great deal of time in Charleston, a place where she now felt deeply isolated.

As she sat in New York, she wondered whether her life was any different from that of the wife of a transferred General Motors employee, who was ripped from her neighborhood and friends and transplanted to a foreign environment. She had been lonely in Wheeling, but she had never felt physically trapped. To compensate,

Rachael packed her schedule in New York with lunches, dinners, and performances. She attended the Metropolitan Opera's performance of Verdi's *Un Ballo in Maschera*, listened to Lorin Maazel conduct Mahler's Fifth Symphony, and saw four plays, including *Dancing at Lughnasa* and *Hear My Song*.

She was tempted to stay longer in New York, but she thought she owed it to Gaston to be with him. He would do the same for her. Recent polls showed he was in serious trouble.

The day after Rachael returned to Charleston, the statehouse press corps staged its annual political spoof, "The Third House."

"It probably was a good thing that Caperton did not bring along the first lady for the performance because Rachael Worby was mercilessly roasted in the skit in which WSAZ's Kathy Young portrayed Worby," wrote one columnist. Singing to the tune of "Mr. Rogers' Neighborhood," Young portrayed Rachael as a patronizing cultural snob, who had little respect for politicians or West Virginians. "The governor works very hard, boys and girls, and he is entitled to a little vacation if peasants, people, keep coming up and tugging at his sleeve and asking him to do something about their wretched road. Can you spell W-H-I-N-E-R-S, boys and girls?" Young sang at one point. "So if the governor is going to get a real rest, he has to go somewhere far, far away where some other governor is supposed to fix the stupid roads. People who don't understand this make me so mad. Can you spell N-I-T-P-I-C-K-E-R-S, boys and girls?"

• • •

Not having a child had been one of the cardinal rules of Rachael's life for years, so much so that, shortly after they married, Gaston, who had two adult sons, had a vasectomy. But in the late autumn, Rachael secretly had started to reconsider her decision, and since then she had thought about having a family nearly every day. The idea unsettled her. Her mother certainly was not a good argument for having children. She had seemed unhappy and frustrated until Rachael and her brothers were older and she returned to school and started working. Her mother, Rachael frequently said, graded herself an A as a mentor and a teacher, a B as a wife, and a C as a mother. Rachael gave her a C-minus, still resentful that she had never seemed to please her mother or meet her expectations.

Her closest friends also weren't great advertisements. When she had looked to them for perspective, she had seen talented, creative women who had checked out of their careers after they had children. One, a cellist, had never finished her dissertation and now refused to spend a night away from home, even though professional musicians had to travel. Another friend gave up her nursing career after the birth of her three children. Rachael felt she could not live without her music. But when a friend, a doctor, told her how he had secretly arranged an adoption as a surprise for his wife after their baby died, Rachael had started to cry. She quietly then had started collecting information about adoptions.

Before she even had raised the subject with Gaston, she had examined her earlier presuppositions. She had wanted to understand, if she could, how she could undergo such a monumental shift. Was it possible that she had not wanted to have a child earlier because her relationships with men had been unstable, and that she only knew now what it was like to have a relationship with someone who was a true partner? Had she wanted a child but been afraid of raising the child alone? She had no physical desire to be pregnant, in part because she had been self-conscious about her appearance on the podium since one of her instructors warned her that her breasts would distract the orchestra. She could not imagine conducting with her stomach sticking out. But didn't this fear suggest something fundamentally wrong? She did not know one woman who didn't want to give birth to her own child. How would she feel about splitting her time between a child and her career? What if she had a chance to spend two weeks touring world-class orchestras while her child was still very young? She would want to go. "Anybody who feels fine about that shouldn't have children," she had told herself.

She had dreaded bringing up the possibility with Gaston because she knew that whatever he might say—yes, no, maybe—would be wrong. If he said, "Fabulous, do," she would think, God, how could you be so blasé about it? Don't you realize what this entails? If he expressed ambivalence, she would feel cheated. He had two sons from his first marriage. How dare he deny her? The only other option was the usual response of older men to younger wives: "If that's what you want, anything you want is just fine with me." In her mind, that would mean he was not involved enough to care. Her imagined reactions reflected her ambivalence and confusion, but she knew she needed to talk to him about it, and finally one Sunday morning in early winter as they lay in bed reading she turned to him. "I want to talk to you about something but not now," she said then. "I want to say something out loud and then I don't want to talk about it. All I want to say is I would like you to be a person who sometimes thinks about the possibility of our adopting a child."

Looking back, she knew she had stunned him. He had tried to question her, but Rachael said she did not want to talk about it then. Gaston meditated every morning, and she wanted him to "just give this some thinking time."

Over the next couple of months, they had talked about babies several times. Gaston focused on the logistics. For every reservation, Rachael had an answer. Could they still have quiet dinners? She pointed out that the mansion was filled with staff who had been urging her to have a baby since the day they married. What about vacations? They could still go, she said. Aware of her impulsive nature and her ability to move mountains when she set her mind to it, he made her promise she would not just pop into the house with a child. He knew she had begun collecting information on adopting. His greatest fear, he told her, was that she and the doctor would go out and get a child and bring it home as a surprise.

She assured him she was not certain she wanted a child. She just wanted him to be open to the idea.

But since the primary had heated up, they recently had agreed to put the discussion on hold, as they had suspended almost everything intimate in their life until the future—after the election. Gaston was gone all day and all night. When they talked they spoke almost exclusively about the campaign. Publicly, she told a *Charleston Daily Mail* reporter, "I never imagined a life as full and satisfying as I have now." Privately, however, she began retreating into herself, withholding more and more of her thoughts. She felt as if their love affair had been put on hold. Each night, she held on to him in bed, telling him how much she missed him.

She told herself they would have a chance to talk more about adopting a child in June, after the primary. They were planning a trip to Italy to stay at the famed Villa d'Este, a luxury resort on Lake Como near Milan. It was the reward she tucked away and brought out when she was feeling particularly low. They would have time together, she could do what she wanted without being scrutinized, and she would be out of Charleston. She could study musical scores; away from the phones and schedules she could accomplish more.

Though she disliked campaigning, Rachael started joining Gaston on the campaign trail, so she could spend more time with him. The long car trips gave them uninterrupted time together, and she visited nearby schools while he made political appearances. A day in Buckhannon and Elkins was typical. After driving together to Buckhannon, he visited the chamber of commerce, senior center and city hall—places where she knew she would bomb—while she spoke at two schools.

She now knew being lower middle class and Jewish in New York was different from being poor and the child of a coal miner in West Virginia. (As a child, she thought being Jewish meant eating chocolate ice cream and getting *The New York Times* in the morning; if you weren't you ate vanilla ice cream and had comics in your newspaper.) But in her speeches to students she almost always focused on the similarities, hoping to inspire them to think big by dispelling the common assumption that she'd had a privileged upbringing.

"My family was blue collar, if that," Worby told students at Buckhannon-Upshur High School. "My father worked in a gas station, my mother did ironing," she said of the family's early years. Though her father did not literally pump gas, he worked at the used car lot affiliated with the station. "With that life, I made this life."

"Everybody in this room has a responsibility to have a dream for yourself. It wasn't talent that got me where I am today," she said, recalling how her parents and teachers all laughed at her ambition to be a conductor. "It was determination and some degree of rebelliousness, too."

Near the end of April, two months into the campaign, Gaston planned a salvage operation to boost Rachael's spirits. He asked the mansion's cook, Otis Laury, to host a small surprise party at Otis's house for Rachael's 43rd birthday, April 21. An eclectic, talented man, Otis was in many ways Rachael's closest friend in Charleston. A native Charlestonian, Otis was unmarried, black, a sculptor, and a music aficionado. They were fellow outsiders, soulmates.

Rachael's eyes filled with tears when the car pulled up

to Otis's home, an arts-and-crafts house that he had renovated himself. Seven guests were waiting. A jazz pianist, a friend, played the piano, and Otis cooked and poured champagne. It was as if Gaston and Otis were trying to recreate a little bit of New York. At dinner, she announced, the night was "perfect," and broke into tears.

A few days later, with barely two weeks to go to the primary, Gaston turned to her as they lay in bed. She could tell by his expression that bad news was about to follow. He said he was going to tell her something that would probably make her mad, but not too mad, he hoped. Rachael waited, her breath quickening. A friend at one of the state's papers had called to ask whether the rumors that he was going to Europe after the primary were true. He said they were. "I'm begging you not to go," he quoted her as saying. "Your opponent will eat you up." People in West Virginia were really hurting. An expensive vacation would look bad, very bad. If they went, she warned, the paper would be unable to defend him.

Gaston paused. "We can't go to Italy."

Rachael did not say anything. She could see from his face that he knew his announcement was like a stake through her heart, and that it demolished him to say it. Rachael could not argue with the logic of Gaston's decision. She realized that Charlotte Pritt, a state legislator who also had entered the Democratic primary, had become a far more formidable opponent than anyone had imagined, surpassing the attorney general and draining support from Gaston. Polls showed that Gaston was only nine points ahead of her. Rachael knew losing would devastate Gaston, but she still could not help feeling "this stinking job." She cried quietly.

The weeks of mounting pressure and scrutiny ate at her. Over the past few days, several people, including women who considered themselves friends, had called Rachael's assistant at the mansion to suggest she change her appearance for the last days of the campaign. But their messages had a uniform ring: "I love Rachael. I love the way she looks. I love the way she dresses, but please just in the last two weeks of the campaign get her to find a really regular suit with a skirt and some pumps." Some suggested something bright or red like Charlotte Pritt's beautiful silk blouses. The comments made Rachael feel awful. Worse, nobody addressed the issue with her in person. Gaston advised her to ignore the meddling, reminding her that she set the standard for what was appropriate. But he was self-confident, unlike her. She had already made one humiliating concession: she had begun shaving the hair on her legs and at her bathing-suit line after one of his Washington political consultants took her aside and warned that visible leg and pubic hairs would offend people. She felt too embarrassed to protest.

Before her marriage, people flocked to her like some wonderful piece of exotica. Her artistic net was coveted. Now she was reduced to pubic hair and blouse problems.

She pulled out a column written a year earlier by the editor of the *Charleston Gazette,* a supporter. "Why do people keep sniping at Rachael Worby?" Don Marsh wrote. "She has had an unusually successful career as a symphony conductor. She is bright. She is attractive. She has brought a lot of good publicity to the state." Marsh chronicled the by now familiar series of criticisms and offered some possible reasons—part of it was a political attack on the governor and part of it was that "she is a person of opinion that she does not attempt to hide."

> I'll offer another reason [he wrote]. She is too vivid; her color is too bright. When I was 12 or so, my father gave me a shotgun. The first day I had it, I went running to the nearest hillside to shoot something.
>
> I saw a number of sparrows but I ignored them. They were too common. Finally a small yellow bird landed on a tree. Its color doomed it.
>
> I killed that bird because it was different and I was ignorant. That was more than 50 years ago, and I still feel bad about it.
>
> Perhaps I shouldn't. What I did may have been wrong, but in wanting to destroy that which was different, I acted in response to my West Virginia heritage.

She had come to the conclusion she was not cut out for political life. She was an artist with an artist's personality—thin-skinned, intense, with well-honed critical faculties. A politician, on the other hand, had to embrace mediocrity to survive and thrive. She hated the idea that she was forced to entrust huge chunks of her future to all these people running Gaston's campaign. The political animal was slow, plodding, inefficient, and insular.

The last week before the primary was hell. After campaigning with Gaston for days, she had two rehearsals scheduled on Sunday for her Thursday concert of *Carmina Burana*, a choral extravaganza based on a secular medieval text written in Latin and German. With a chorus of 125 adults and 50 children, the coordination was enough to make Rachael anxious. To add to the pressure, her publicist and agent were flying in from New York for the performance. After rehearsals, she flew back to Charleston for last-minute campaigning. On Monday, she flew to six different cities for campaign rallies. She was a nervous wreck.

On Tuesday, Gaston won the primary, and the attorney general conceded at 10 P.M. Pritt, however, refused to concede and accused Gaston's campaign of voter fraud. She threatened to be his "little hellion," his "fatal attraction," and said she was considering a write-in campaign. Rachael was horrified, but she remained silent at the suggestion of Gaston's advisers, who thought Pritt would sound crazier if no one responded. Victory in the Democratic primary should mean almost certain victory in West Virginia, an overwhelmingly Democratic state, but the former governor had been a Republican and Rachael noted grimly that nothing was certain.

On Thursday, Rachael performed her concert, and the following morning she met with her agent and publicist for breakfast. Rachael had grown accustomed to the praise of her friends and her husband, the applause of her audiences in Wheeling, but they did not count in her mind because they did not have sophisticated musical ears. But these two women were different. Agnes Eisenberger, her agent, and Mary Lou Falcone, her publicist, were at the top of their profession in the classical music world. Rachael was convinced they had taken her on as a charity case or a lark.

Falcone, a tall, strong-looking woman with a direct manner, had never heard Rachael conduct in Wheeling. She spoke first. The performance was terrific, she said. Rachael had decoded the score and made it shine. The musicians played together with great sensitivity and attention to detail. Altogether, the concert had affirmed Falcone's decision to work with Rachael, a judgment some of her colleagues had questioned because Rachael did not have the stature of her other clients. Rachael had obviously taken an orchestra that was at the bottom of the heap and made it into a very, very fine regional orchestra. Eisenberger agreed.

Next, both women said they wanted to talk about areas she needed to improve. On the podium she was riveting and powerful, they said, but her walk from offstage to the podium was apologetic. She was too inclusive of the orchestra during bows, stepping down among the musicians and making herself seem one of them. She jumped too quickly onto the podium. Her manner did not say to the audience, you're mine. Conducting was still a man's world. As a petite woman with an angelic pretty face, she had to act stronger to be taken seriously.

She also did not appear to be taking herself seriously enough, they said. When she visited other symphonies to watch rehearsals, she should go backstage and introduce herself to the conductors. She was a leader on the podium, but she needed to be a leader offstage, too.

Finally, they said they wanted to talk to her about complaints they had heard when they called other orchestras to solicit guest-conducting appearances for her. These invitations were crucial because an orchestra usually hired someone as its music director only after several guest appearances. No one complained about

Rachael's skill as a musician, they said, but many complained about her laserlike criticism. "We hear she's difficult with musicians, that she is harsh and critical" was one comment. She had a reputation, they continued, as someone who tended to fixate on mistakes rather than accomplishments.

Rachael did not disagree. She could be very sarcastic and unforgiving during rehearsals, and she had gotten rid of a number of the original members of the Wheeling Symphony by forcing them to see they couldn't play well, which undoubtedly had been humiliating for them. But no one got the results she got without being tough. Besides, she thought the complaints were outdated. She hadn't been that way for two years, she said. She thought she had toned down her criticisms and softened significantly in the past year and a half.

"You are a perfectionist," Falcone said, warning her that she was setting herself up for failure because perfection was unattainable. She could not absolutely control 100 people. "You aren't their mouth. You aren't their fingers. If they blow wrong or push down on the wrong note, you can't blame them," she said. Rachael needed to strive for excellence but she could not be a perfectionist on the podium.

"In the old days," she continued, "no one would have taken exception to what you demand, but the days of von Karajan and Toscanini are over." Conductors could no longer be screaming tyrants because musicians now had a large say in selecting conductors.

It was hard enough as it was to get her abilities recognized, a process that was already part timing and part luck. Rachael also carried the additional baggage of being known primarily as a conductor of young people's concerts. She was considered tops in that category, but if Rachael wanted to be the music director of a major American symphony, as she insisted repeatedly, she needed to help them by softening her edges.

Rachael inquired about an opening with the Alabama Symphony. Eisenberger told her that was too small a move. Carnegie Hall already provided her with wonderful visibility. Stay focused on your work in Wheeling and continue to produce excellent results. Learn scores, Eisenberger said. Enhance your German, your Italian. Proficiency in languages would help in Europe. She had a lot of work to do, but the right opportunity would come along, and she would be ready for it.

They told her to stop worrying about the jobs she did not get or which colleagues were surpassing her. They were both aware that the rejections devastated her and she became inconsolable, retreating to her room in a flood of tears, unable to study or listen to music. She had told both at different times in the past few years that she had thought about quitting conducting because she felt stagnant, that she would never amount to anything. But she also knew she could not live without music. She couldn't imagine what she would do. She would just sort of lie down and be still for the rest of her life.

This was unproductive thinking, they told her, and only added to her despair. Everybody gets rejected, they said. Stay put and mind your manners, just pick yourself up off the ground and move on when rejected.

She pledged to try.

Rachael felt unexpectedly optimistic after the meeting. Normally, she would hear only the criticisms and lock herself in her room crying: There were no prospects for future jobs. There were no imminent guest-conducting positions. In essence, they had told her they were having a hard time finding her work. But this time what she also heard was that they believed in her deeply and were committed to her, even if it meant passing on bad news. They wanted to help her, but she needed to hold on.

In the midst of struggling with the question of her own professional standing, Rachael had the added burden of political reality—her other life. Gaston wanted to take off the weekend after the primary to rest. Because any trip outside the state might draw headlines, they headed to the Greenbrier, a posh golfing resort in the heart of West Virginia, but hardly a place to find privacy. Guests almost knocked her down to say hello to the governor. Embarrassed, Gaston then pressed her in front of him. "You know Rachael, don't you?" he'd say. Rachael scheduled a massage. But she carefully taped a Band-Aid over a small tattoo on her upper thigh—something from her earlier life—before going for the massage. Gaston said her caution was unnecessary, but she had learned otherwise.

As she thought about the primary, she began to feel worse about the previous ten weeks. She wanted her old life back, free from scrutiny. In her eyes, Gaston was a miracle worker as governor, but she could not help feeling she was being disparaged in the process.

She'd taken recently to examining other political wives for some guidance, but she just came away feeling even more like a black sheep. Hillary Clinton did not seem to think she was sacrificing anything. A few days after the primary, Rachael read in *The New York Times* that Hillary had said she was more like Barbara Bush than unlike her. "Barbara Bush and I have a lot in common," Clinton told the reporter. "We're both committed women. We care very deeply about our families; we're supportive of our husbands." Rachael almost dropped the paper. The remark made her sick. It was a sellout. "Am I the only one left who is going to be myself?" she asked. "Am I the only feminist left?"

Rachael had strong interests that could be called political in the broadest definition—she was an advocate for the arts and education and was outspoken in her support of abortion and gay rights—and initially political work had seemed exciting, even romantic. But that was from a distance. Now she felt being first lady more and more split her life.

During the primary she had stayed in Charleston for much longer stretches than normal because her absences might draw criticism, but a week after the primary she returned to New York for ten days. She had a series of concerts at Carnegie Hall, the culmination of her in-school performances, and she was starved for cultural diversions. She wanted to see a foreign movie with subtitles. In Charleston, when she decided to polish her German, she couldn't even find Berlitz in the phone book. They were small petty problems, but manifestations of real issues. The only place she felt she was truly happy was in New York.

But even New York did not provide a complete escape. She asked Gaston to attend one of her Carnegie Hall concerts and to stay after the program for an important fundraising luncheon. Four hundred people had each donated $500 a plate for the program. As she entered the dining room, one of the Carnegie Hall assistants asked if she minded splitting up from Gaston. She said she did not. Then she noticed that Gaston was squired around to meet a number of prominent people in the room and guided to the table of honor to be seated between the violinist Isaac Stern, a man she desperately wanted to cultivate, and Brooke Astor, one of the country's leading patrons of the arts. When Rachael found her table, the organizer of the event rose. "Mrs. Caperton, what a pleasure it is to have you here." It was clear from comments the woman later made that she had no idea that Rachael, who had released her hair from her concert bun, was also the conductor.

She had another concert the following day. The lights dimmed and the audience hushed. Rachael skipped onto the stage, bowed, and immediately commanded the orchestra with a tip of her hand to play "Fanfare for a Common Man." "It is always such a treat for me to hear the brass," she said when the piece was finished. "Whenever I close my eyes and listen it conjures up images of castles. The truth about music is that you don't have to dream up a building. Every piece of music has its own form." Warm and engaging, she used architectural concepts to explain the importance of structure to music. Leaping from the stage to the aisle in front of the seats, moving constantly through the hall, one moment she was conducting the orchestra, another she was asking questions of the audience. "Has anyone in this hall imagined square water?" she asked, and the hands shot up in the audience. One boy mentioned a fish aquarium, another an ice cube. Rachael then held up a cinder block.

"Another way to think of music is to imagine cement taking form. Music isn't really liquid in the way water or cement is, but when music is not in a container it can sound cacophonous." She waved to the orchestra to play randomly. "Enough, enough," she shouted in mock horror. A prominent architect, Hugh Hardy, joined her on the stage, illustrating the similarities between music and buildings by drawing colorful computerized sketches that were displayed on a big overhead screen. For one hour, the kids seemed enthralled.

After her last concert on Friday, she returned to Charleston. She had a day to set up one of her arts lectures, scheduled at the mansion for Sunday, along with a reception for 200 bicyclists.

Because the campaign schedule allowed few escapes from Charleston before the general election, Rachael decided to follow her agent's and publicist's advice to spend most of her free time in June studying. She had no concerts until her July 4 series, and she promised herself she was going to act constructively rather than concentrate on her disappointment. She had new scores to learn, as well as her German.

As part of her effort to keep her cool, she carefully planned her week at the Democratic National Convention in New York in the middle of July to make sure it had balance. She knew she would blow up if she did nothing but attend the convention. She studied German in the mornings and scheduled meetings in the afternoons at Carnegie Hall to plan her upcoming season. She picked out a couple of high-profile convention events at which to make appearances. The plotting paid off. Instead of feeling she had wasted her time, she felt she had accomplished a great deal. She had secured Arthur Mitchell of the Dance Theater of Harlem to be her guest performer at Carnegie Hall after meeting with him for four hours.

Once the convention was over, she decided to mend and build some political fences. It would be good for Gaston and therefore good for her. She had made herself too vulnerable by taking the political slights too personally. She started first with Jay and Sharon Rockefeller, who had finally agreed to host a fundraiser for Gaston during the first week of August. She wrote Sharon Rockefeller telling her how much she admired her work and included a T-shirt for one of their children.

Next were the Clintons. Rachael was suspicious of Bill Clinton and found Hillary cold and distant, an impression formed in part after talking to some of the Clintons' state troopers at a governors' association meeting. But Gaston and the Arkansas governor were friends, and Rachael secretly hoped that Gaston might get a cabinet appointment if Clinton won and Gaston lost. She could work on the friendship. That's how things happened, she joked to friends. When the Clintons and Al and Tipper Gore swung through West Virginia on their bus tour after the convention, Rachael joined the trip and urged Hillary to be herself and ignore the right-wing attacks on her as a career woman. Baking cookies and handing out her recipe was a mistake, she told Hillary, describing how she had resisted suggestions that she cut her hair or stop wearing sunglasses. "Women in America like you for what you are," she said, realizing she needed to listen to her own advice.

But as she moved through the end of July and August, her words of reassurance became increasingly hollow as the jabs intensified. When a newspaper poll tabulated that 50 percent of those interviewed believed Rachael should refer to herself as Rachael Caperton, not Worby and only 24 percent said they had no trouble with her keeping her name, she threw the paper down on her desk in disgust. Still, there were some things she refused to ignore. After she read a fundraising letter for a state politician that mentioned that his opponent, who had a Jewish last name, was being supported by Hollywood and New York money, she thought the reference was subtly anti-Semitic and as a Jew could not ignore it. At the Rockefeller fundraiser, she approached the politician. He told her he didn't have anything to do with the letter. "That's really wonderful," Gaston later said sarcastically when she told him about the conversation. He understood her feelings, he said, but the last thing he needed was a fight with one of the state's politicians.

Still, she was overwhelmed with things she thought she should do. A thousand people were expected at the mansion August 9 to listen to an opera singer as part of her arts series. She had accepted dozens of invitations for state and campaign events, and she was still trying to raise money for her literacy foundation as well as participate in the search for a new dean at a state university. Her big free outdoor concerts were coming up. She attended a Mozart concert for diversion and instruction, but she realized at the end she had been thinking about everything except music.

Exasperated and exhausted, she told her assistant what Sharon Rockefeller had said: that when she had been the state's first lady, she had attended only high-profile events with guaranteed media coverage. That was what Rachael wanted to do now. She handed her assistant a paragraph she had written, explaining why she had to decline a request, and instructed her assistant to put it on the computer and use it in reply to future requests. In practice, however, Rachael found her own rule almost impossible to follow. She believed she had an obligation to use her platform as first lady for otherwise neglected causes. If she did not organize for AIDS or get books donated to the library, she believed no one else would. After touring one state college and finding its arts curriculum lacking, she insisted on joining the search committee for a new dean of the arts department. The college president resisted, saying it was not customary to include people from outside the university. "It's time for a change," Rachael replied.

She had seen the success she could have when she had filmed two public-service announcements in the spring, urging West Virginians to give their moms mammograms for Mother's Day. Health clinics and hospitals offered free mammograms to women who were uninsured or underinsured, and she helped write the scripts for the commercials. She arranged for television stations to air them, and then tracked their appearances. It was hard to turn her back on the kind of influence she could have in a small state. Change always seemed within her grasp.

At the same time, she could sense that Gaston's staff and political allies were becoming increasingly resistant to her. Her assistant recently had reported that Gaston's campaign staff had tried to discourage her from attending a meeting to discuss Gaston's schedule, even though Rachael had told her assistant to sit in. "It's my life even if they don't think it's important," Rachael said. "You should go. You need to represent me." After the meeting was over, her assistant told her that no one seemed to be aware of Rachael's concerns. In fact the staff had gone further. One of Gaston's aides complained that if Rachael did not like being at a campaign event she showed it. The aide cited a campaign event the previous weekend that had flopped because the governor and Rachael left early, at what she thought was clearly Rachael's insistence.

Her idea to raise funds later that month for the scores of people left homeless in Florida by Hurricane Andrew was met with similar reluctance. Her projects always required a lot of work, she was told, and there were not enough people to help her. The reaction from Gaston's political advisers to her next suggestion was even worse. She said she planned to send out a plain Christmas card announcing that a contribution had been made in the recipient's name to the Pediatric AIDS Foundation. That was a better use of the huge amount of money they had spent last year sending out elaborate cards. "I'd rather do something else with our money," she said. AIDS was too controversial, Gaston's advisers told her. Why raise an issue that was not in the forefront of most West Virginians' minds? People framed Christmas cards from the governor. Initially, she protested. People were dying of AIDS, including people in West Virginia. Privately, she said to herself, "Not only am I having to think about Christmas cards, but I have to think about the political ramifications of a Christmas card. I'm not even Christian." Tired of fighting but also aware that it was not fair to Gaston to cause him unnecessary controversy, she folded. It was his job, after all.

• • •

As hard as it was for her to imagine, the campaign pace picked up in September. She began getting up at 5 a.m. so she could practice the harpsichord. She was scheduled to accompany her guest performers at the end of the month, and she thought she needed to campaign with Gaston, even though he urged her to spend her time on her music. But she could not be dissuaded, and practicing early in the morning was the only way to keep her anger about the campaign from eating into her music.

It was not the time to pull back from her music. The orchestra was performing at its peak level—she could not believe it was the Wheeling Symphony Orchestra— and she had applied for an opening with the symphony in Little Rock, Arkansas, a well-respected regional orchestra. She believed she had a good shot. In a period when many symphonies across the country were struggling, she now had shown six straight years of growth and major improvements in Wheeling. The orchestra performed with musical grace and lyricism. A board looking for a new conductor would have to be impressed.

She still spent too much time that month fuming over press criticism. Even if there had been a time when she did not read state newspapers, she did now, especially when one of Gaston's friends called to tell her to ignore a negative article, as almost always happened. In mid-September, she blew up at a column by L. T. Anderson in the *Daily Mail* that accused her of improperly using her position as first lady to secure state money for her literacy foundation, alleging that two-thirds of the funds had come from the state. As far as she was concerned, the column was just another in a long line of personal attacks by Anderson. He had been picking on her since the day she married Gaston. She wanted him to stop. Should she have lunch with him? she asked a friend. Should she write his editor? Should she talk to the publisher? She was worried about the cumulative effect his attacks might have on her as a musician, but she said what really bothered her was that Anderson seemed to be on a personal vendetta against her. His columns were read by everyone in Charleston, and she did not like being a subject of constant ridicule.

In defensive moods like this, Rachael usually was incapable of self-examination. She believed that if her actions were well intentioned the recipients naturally would welcome her help. Stamping out illiteracy and rescuing the state from the cultural backwaters were noble and enlightened goals in her mind. It didn't occur to her that citing the large number of people in grocery stores who asked her to read labels to them as evidence of the need for her literacy campaign might come off as arrogant or condescending to West Virginians. "I have never been asked to read a label to someone," Anderson wrote then. Rachael could not see that Anderson might speak for others in the state who might take exception to suggestions that they were inadequate, or that they might have different sensibilities from hers and resent her attempts to impose her own. Instead, she brooded about the column for days. She called the publisher of the *Daily Mail* to schedule a meeting to lay out her complaints.

Sitting in his office, she argued that the columnist had been on her case for months for no apparent reason. His antipathy, she said, did not appear to be political, because he was soft on her husband. When the publisher asked whether she might have done something to spark his personal ire, Rachael said she had never met him. "I can understand him hating me because I'm short, or because I'm Jewish . . . or because I won't change my name to Caperton, or I have a career," she said. She wasn't there to say Anderson should not write about her. She was a public figure. But his attacks were unfair. She asked him to intervene.

To her surprise, a few days later the publisher ran an open letter to Worby in the paper: "Rachael Worby, we like you at the *Daily Mail.* We really do." After reviewing 16 columns the columnist had written about her, the publisher said he agreed with Rachael's assessment. The columnist "appears not to like her and has taken every opportunity to let people know that. I think some of the shots he has taken have been off the mark and even in poor taste." Someone had finally heard her.

The reprieve was short lived. Ten days later, a columnist at the *Sunday Gazette-Mail* of Charleston reported that Rachael had mistreated some of the state troopers assigned to protect her and the governor. She had kicked one state trooper during a helicopter ride, the story said, and cursed another at the governor's mansion after she missed a phone call. Papers all over the state picked up the story. Rachael was in Canada to watch another conductor rehearse when the story broke. To her fury, Gaston and his aides counseled her to keep quiet. A response would only prolong the story—and divert attention from the campaign. But she maintained, and a witness verified, that the only action she had taken with her foot was a nervous nudging of the trooper's knee to urge him to ask the pilot why the helicopter had started to lurch violently. As for the other trooper, she said she had sworn at him in a loud voice, but she had done so only after discovering that she had missed an important phone call from one of Gaston's aides. Furious because she had been waiting all day for the call, she blasted the trooper for not making a better effort to find her. Besides, she said, he had used coarse language with her, too, when he told her he searched every room for her.

"They are trying to do a Hillary Clinton on me," she complained to friends, referring to the way Hillary Clinton had been seemingly forced to retreat from her prominent independent role in the campaign. Suspicious that she was being sacrificed for the campaign, Rachael nonetheless deferred to the campaign aides' wishes and refused to answer questions about the story the day after she returned to West Virginia to keep a long-standing commitment to campaign for a friend in Jefferson County, touring five service agencies and a women's shelter.

Privately, however, she continued to rail. Gaston's comments to the press—"Rachael is my greatest asset"—seemed weak; they reminded her of Michael Dukakis's bloodless response to a 1988 presidential debate question about how he would react if his wife were raped and murdered. No one was really defending her. No one was saying it wasn't true. She knew, however, that if she didn't act the kicking story would stick to her like an indelible stain, forever part of her public description, like her not reading state newspapers. What orchestra board would want to hire someone who kicked her employees? Still brooding, she contacted a lawyer and said she wanted to sue the papers for libel.

The next day Gaston and his aides rallied to her defense and issued a statement from the trooper whom she had allegedly kicked. He confirmed her description of the incident and described media accounts as "untrue and unfair." "Being familiar with the first lady's concerns about flying in small craft, I understood her behavior to be that of a frightened passenger and in no way any kind of physical abuse," the trooper said. But that was four days after the story broke, and her feeling of abandonment lingered. No one had considered the ruinous impact the stories might have on her applications for orchestral positions. Gaston's advisers were treating her strictly as Rachael, wife of candidate. She was looking at the stories as Rachael, candidate for conductorships with other bigger symphonies. Hillary Clinton put up with the barbs and criticisms because her bread-and-butter was politics, like her husband's; a few months of softening her image was a small price to pay to reach the White House. Rachael was an artist. Music, not politics, ran through her veins.

She felt helpless, and reacted defensively, unable to see the discomfort a trooper might feel when nudged with her foot, however innocently, or understand that her temper might have ignited the outburst by the other trooper. The warm side of her personality was generous to a fault. But the temperamental side blew at the slightest imperfection in times of crisis, unmasking a large blind spot. She had little understanding of how abrasive or insulting her rebukes could be, or that stories like this circulated because people had come to expect a degree of arrogance from her, regardless of whether the specifics were true.

Charlotte Pritt, meanwhile, had decided to wage an independent write-in campaign, and called a press conference in Wheeling. She suggested that the state fared better with a first lady like the former governor's wife, who had gracious manners. "Most people don't understand Rachael very well. I don't know her, either, and don't know for sure what to think," Pritt said. "She seems very different. I don't know what to make of such an exotic bird." If elected, Pritt promised not to treat state troopers "as if they were down on the plantation. . . . I don't think state employees should be treated as servants," a not so subtle reference to the fact that one of the allegedly mistreated troopers was black.

The day after Pritt's remarks, Rachael left West Virginia for a one-day escape to Washington. From the airport she called a member of the symphony board in Little Rock, Arkansas, who was shepherding her application for an opening there. He told her that some of his board colleagues doubted that she could commit sufficient time to the symphony, given her political obligations in West Virginia. "How can the first lady of West Virginia take care of us down here in Little Rock with the Arkansas Symphony?" was their biggest question, he said. Rachael said, "Tell them to look at my track records and they'll see where my priorities lie." Since her arrival, the number of subscribers had tripled, her budget had quadrupled, and the number of performances had increased from 5 to 37. He said he had done that, but some board members were unimpressed, chalking up her success to her marriage to Gaston. "Of course you would be able to make an orchestra grow like that in West Virginia. That's where you're the first lady," he said some had concluded.

Rachael hung up the phone, feeling beat up, pessimistic, and stuck. If she couldn't get consideration in Arkansas, where could she? She felt she was being robbed of her ability to make music in peace in West Vir-

ginia, and she couldn't make music outside of West Virginia. One way or another being married to the governor
was proving to be a liability for her own professional aspirations. When people asked her if her life as first lady
was like she expected it to be, she said she would never
have guessed that marrying Gaston would get in the way
of her ability to expand her career or be used by people
as a means of discounting her as a conductor. If anything, she had thought, it might be tantalizing and work
as an asset.

In the old days, after a phone call like this she would
have canceled her trip and returned, crying, to her bed-
room. But she was trying to handle rejection more maturely since her May meeting with her agent and her
publicist, and she boarded the plane, forcing herself to
study her scores as she flew to Washington. Once there,
she reviewed the scores for several more hours and then
called Gaston to give him an update about the Arkansas
job. She joked that they would have to get a divorce. She
did not mean it. She had never needed or loved anyone
as she loved Gaston, and no one had ever returned the
support or love he gave her daily. But she was at the end
of her rope.

Her comments obviously pained him, and he told her
he knew how hard the campaign had been on her. They
needed to figure out what to do, he said, because the last
thing he ever wanted was to stand in her way. Privately,
he had begun to wonder whether he had done Rachael a
favor in marrying her. Politics and the campaign had
meant time away from her music. It was degrading to her.

On November 3, 1992, Gaston coasted to victory with
an ease that led the CBS *Evening News* to announce his
reelection just ten minutes after the polls closed. Rachael

was relieved that they would finally get some freedom and time together. After living through hell, she felt it was a victory and vindication of sorts, too. And at last, the criticism would stop. Rachael told a news reporter: "When you (super) impose being married to Gaston onto my life as a musician it's rather hectic, but I am happy. My life proceeds forward at a pace that surprises even me."

Over the next two months, Rachael was out of the state for 37 days.

Nearly four months after Gaston's reelection, in late February 1993, and nearly two years after we first spoke, Rachael and Gaston arrived in Washington for the weekend. The ostensible purpose was to celebrate Gaston's birthday, but the real motivation seemed to be to give Rachael a boost—an extended time away from West Virginia. Gaston's reelection had not brought the reprieve she had much anticipated.

She had worked intensely on Gaston's inaugural festivities in January. Overseeing the smallest of details, she chose the color of the plywood stage and helped design the invitations. She opened the celebration by conducting the Wheeling Symphony in a commemorative concert, an event meant to symbolize the marriage of their lives. But the most talked-about story from the inauguration was that she did not bow her head during the invocation prayer, and appeared to be "making eyes at someone in the crowd," according to one local account.

"I didn't receive any credit for working hard or for the

fact that more handicapped people than ever were able to come," she complained.

She had taken another hit a few days later in a long profile in the *Sunday Gazette-Mail*, Charleston's Sunday paper. The story recounted a reporter's trip with Rachael to her favorite Wheeling restaurant, Ye Olde Alpha, where Rachael asked the owner, one of her first symphony sponsors, what he thought about the coming state-sponsored video lottery machines. He asked her to help him get ten of the machines. According to the story, she told him she would help him because he had helped her in the past by buying concert seats. "If I get you these things, though, I'll get you to buy more seats," she said, according to the paper.

The conversation had been tape-recorded and the reporter later asked Rachael if it appeared she might be performing a favor for a friend. "How do you think people get things?" the reporter quoted her saying. "What? Are you kidding me? How do you think people in this state get things? How do people anywhere get things? Through friends. You have a friend in the Senate who's on the finance committee. Guess what happens? You get something. You have an enemy . . . on the finance committee. Guess what happens? You get nothing. That's what friends are for. I should hope my friends would, from time to time, call on me for something special." Rachael was in New York on one of her musical tours of city schools when the story ran, leaving Gaston to quell the firestorm. He explained, to almost universal disbelief, that Rachael had been joking, an assertion that even his closest friends found hard to believe. "I would hate to be you," one of them said to Rachael when she returned to Charleston. "There are so many people who dislike you. I couldn't stand it."

"I think I might be the most-hated first lady in the history of the state," she said, looking out the window as snow fell. "I might even be the most-hated first lady in the country."

Her life, she said, had become unbearable in West Virginia. She said she did not seem to be able to leave the mansion without generating a negative story. One of her most persistent critics, she said, had been calling around all week to check on a story that she had told off a couple of college football players attending a reception at the mansion. Rachael said she had bumped into them wandering around the governor's private quarters and asked them to leave. "I was dressed, but I often walk around in a T-shirt and underwear," she said. "I was nice about it."

She knew she should be able to shake off the criticism, but it still made her despondent despite all the advice to ignore it. When she read a funny retort in *New York Magazine* from the subject of a negative profile she said, "I wanted to call him up and say, Can I come to your school?"

She laughed but then quickly grew somber. "I told Gaston I did not want to live in West Virginia anymore," she said. "No one likes me." I asked if there was a solution. "They're all extreme," she answered. She wanted him to resign, move to New York. But that, she knew, was impossible and absurd. Gaston had just been re-elected. But she wanted him to at least understand the depths of her feelings. "I asked him how he would feel if we moved to Israel and lived in a religious community where no one liked him?"

After two years of following Rachael's life, I knew

some West Virginians disliked her intensely. Some of it was unfair, some of it political. A certain amount was the defensive posturing of people who felt belittled by Rachael's efforts to improve them. And some of it was also Rachael's fault. She had a tendency to pop people right in their most vulnerable spot or to make comments without thinking through their repercussions.

Contrary to her assessment, however, the criticism was not universal. I had traveled to Charleston a few months earlier and spent part of one morning white-water rafting with Rachael and a group of West Virginians. Shortly after finishing our run, a chunky middle-aged blond man approached Rachael, almost trembling. He clutched her hand, "You are my wife's heroine." His wife's mother had always wanted to be a conductor, he said, but had had to settle for playing the organ in her basement.

There was something else Rachael wanted to add. In late December, she said, her mother called to report that she had just received the invitation which Rachael had helped design. Rachael felt her breath quicken as she listened to her mother on the phone. "I am overwhelmed with you," her mother told her. "There is no woman I admire more in the world. You're a conductor. You're a first lady." Rachael imagined her mother running her fingers over the navy-blue invitation, imprinted with gold ink, its pages separated by fine translucent paper and tied together with flaxen thread. "It has your imprimatur all over it," she said her mother continued, her own words rushing together with emotion. The invitation listed both the inaugural and Rachael's concert.

Her mother paused and Rachael said she sensed confusion in her mother's voice. "But there is one question I want to ask you. What happened?" What change, she said her mother wanted to know, had taken place since her childhood? "You were such a nothing all your childhood," she said, Rachael recalled. She was stunned as her mother reeled off names of seventh-grade peers who had been superior to Rachael in nearly every category. One had been a wonderful pianist, better than Rachael. "You couldn't play the piano like that," Rachael quoted her. Rachael's voice quickened as she repeated the conversation, listing the more talented friends her mother mentioned. Thirty years had passed, but her mother seemed to have perfect recall of her classmates' names, almost as good as Rachael's.

Rachael said she knew her mother intended the contrast as a compliment: Rachael had achieved something significant in her life. But Rachael heard only the negative side. "Gee, Mom, I don't know," she responded meekly. Her mother pressed.

Rachael stumbled. "Maybe it all started when I married Gaston," she said in almost a whisper, quoting herself. "He loves me. He makes me feel better about myself. He gives me the confidence to do other things." The jab at her mother was obvious.

Her mother, she said, snapped with exasperation, "Oh, come on. We loved you."

Rachael hung up the phone, feeling numb. "A nothing," she said.

Rachael certainly had commented several times in our interviews over the years that her mother was overly critical of her, both as a child and as a young adult, but I realized now that the conflict between her work and her role as first lady—my original journalistic framework—was secondary in importance to her deep-seated and unresolved issues with her mother. The rendering of her upbringing was Rachael's version; I hadn't heard her mother's. But what mattered was that Rachael had always felt her mother was condemning her. To her, this was the truth. Her mother had spoken in the past tense, but her judgment cut like a knife.

"I felt like I was in a coma," Rachael said. She was still a nothing, driven to gain her mother's approval and love, unable to take control of her own life because her identity and sense of self were intertwined with her mother's assessments. As long as she felt loved in proportion to her achievements, she would continue to confuse admiration with love and seek public adulation to build her self-esteem. When praise was withheld—by the press, symphony boards, political allies, or friends—the criticism was a reminder, and validation, of her mother's earlier assessments. "I didn't want to have to be nobody," I found written in my notes when I returned to them to check her reaction to the advice of Gaston's staff not to respond to the allegations about kicking the trooper. I turned to the pages describing her reaction to job rejections. "I'm never going to be anybody," she had said, explaining the devastation. "The rejection negates me as a whole person," she had added. All nothings. The easy collapse of her self-esteem was proof of just how precarious it was. That was why she reacted so strongly.

"What about having a child?" I asked. Did her feelings about her relationship with her mother have anything to do with this? She took a breath and looked away. "I am going to tell you something I've never told anyone," she began haltingly.

She had her public excuses for putting off having a child and even some private ones that she'd shared with me and Gaston, but she also had a secret one, she said. When she thought about adopting a child she sometimes thought, "Now my mother will really love me because I've finally done something she approves of." But then, she said, her voice growing quieter, "I really worry, 'What if I have a child and then a year later my mother calls and she still thinks I'm a nothing?' " What would she do then? she asked, the hope draining out of her voice.

A nothing, again. Because her mother's approval still counted so much, she had difficulty not only in creating her own identity, but she also did not have a clear-eyed view about having a child. She could not separate her desire, or lack of it, from what her mother might think about her having a child.

A few moments later, Gaston came into the room and said they needed to leave to make it back before the small Charleston airport closed for lack of visibility. The snow was beginning to fall heavily and a plane must pass over a mountain range and drop rapidly and precipitously in order to hit the runway there. It was frightening even in the mildest weather.

Rachael picked up her tennis shoes and left the room. A few moments later I found her sitting on the bottom stair, tightening her laces and crying. Her mascara was smeared. "I don't want to go home. I'm so unhappy there. I don't want to go back," she whispered. Gaston, who had reentered the house, looked pained and reached out to take her hand. As he walked with his arm around her shoulder, they slipped into the backseat of the waiting trooper's car.

Alison's
STORY

Dr. Alison Estabrook, a surgeon at Columbia-Presbyterian Medical Center in New York City, sliced through the tissue of the patient who lay unconscious on the operating table, carefully avoiding the sinewy nerves. The hiss of flesh being cauterized and the soft swishing of the anesthesiology pump filled the air. Though she had been a full-time surgeon at the hospital for nearly two years, Alison, 34, had spent six years in training there, and the young doctor assisting at her elbow was peppering her with questions about what it was like to be a staff surgeon. Columbia was the second-largest hospital in the country, affiliated with a top university, and one of the most prestigious research facilities in the world. Only the best, or so it was thought, had a shot at being asked to join the staff. The assistant was a resident nearing the end of surgical training at Columbia, and looking for a job.

What was her starting salary? he asked. Alison had a strong athletic build and wore standard-issue pale blue surgical pants and top with her shoulder-length red hair tucked under a cap. She looked almost indistinguishable from the resident, except for the positioning of the V-neck, which she had started wearing backward after she noticed an anesthesiologist peering at her cleavage when she bent over a patient.

No one had asked Alison about her salary before, but she knew the resident's wife was a teacher and they were planning to have a child. He probably would be the sole provider.

"Sixty thousand dollars," she answered. A look of puzzlement registered on the resident's face, and Alison thought he must have misheard her. Even without a surgical mask to muffle her words, she spoke with a slight nasal tone and often in quick spurts of phrases that sometimes she had to repeat.

"Alison," he said, pronouncing her name with exaggeration. She lifted her eyes from her patient to peer briefly at him. They had worked many long hours together and shared the offbeat humor that often develops between people working under arduous conditions, but Alison immediately sensed a change in his tone. "I can't believe the difference in your salaries," he said.

"What do you mean?" she asked, her back straightening.

The two other surgeons hired from her residency class had been hired at about $100,000 a year, he said. In case she might have missed the point, he added, "Do you know these guys are making $40,000 more than you?" The hospital was "really pulling the wool over your eyes," he said.

The resident made some joke that she was an idiot for not negotiating a better deal, but his words were lost on Alison, who had withdrawn into a furious internal dialogue. She had undergone the same training as these two other surgeons. She had published several papers and won the coveted Blakemore award for outstanding research, the only award that was represented by a plaque in the department of surgery offices. They had started their residencies and ended them on the same day. Their employment as staff surgeons had begun on exactly the same day, July 1, 1984, yet they were making 60 percent more money than Alison.

Why was this happening? she asked herself. What was the reasoning behind it? There had to be an explanation. Were these guys doing more complicated surgery? Were they bringing in a lot more money? Maybe they are much better deal makers than I am.

It never even crossed her mind to negotiate when she had gone to her superiors in the fourth year of her residency to ask if she was going to be offered a job. Her husband, a resident in pathology named Bill Harrington, still had several years to go at Columbia and staying would make life much easier. Her superiors had just said this is your salary and you have the privilege of working at great Columbia-Presbyterian. She loved the sense of mastery and competence she had in the operating room, and surgery fit her personality. She was dexterous—with a skill developed in childhood from helping her father build ham radios and train sets—and she liked to make decisions quickly, a requirement for a surgeon. The job offer was proof that she had succeeded. Besides, it also meant she and her husband could buy a house.

Not once had she questioned the salary, she thought,

tossing off her surgical clothes in the locker room. She was still berating herself when she pulled into her driveway in Englewood, New Jersey, twenty minutes later. The dark two-story house, with its graceful sloping roof and leaded windows, set on two acres of lush, gardens, usually calmed her after a chaotic day amid the grime and blight of Columbia's impoverished neighborhood. But this evening Alison whisked past the flowers and the towering tomato plants that Bill, a dedicated gardener, cultivated.

"I have been a fool," she said, the transformation of her confusion into anger complete. The only difference she told herself was that the two other surgeons were men.

Alison recounted her discovery to Bill. "This is an outrage," he exploded. Bill was not the passionate type, but he was solid, dependable—the partner she had been seeking when she married him. The madly-in-love, wonderfully sexual relationships always seemed to end in major unhappiness for her, as had the one with her last boyfriend, a doctor who'd pestered her to switch to a less time-consuming field, like dermatology, and convert to Judaism. Bill, who was specializing in the pathology of brain tumors, was the opposite. He liked who she was and endorsed her choices. Although her friends might not think it terribly romantic or ideal, that attitude allowed her to be herself, without thinking or fighting. The trade-off was worth it.

Bill urged her to contact a labor-relations lawyer, but Alison knew that Bill's first instinct usually was to fight, a tendency Alison did not share. Her mother, Shirley, would give her calmer advice. Her mother had always worked full time, first as a writer for *Fortune* and *Time* magazines, and then later as one of the founders of *Peo-*

ple magazine. She was now copublisher of a small Rhode Island newspaper. Work, her mother had taught Alison and her two sisters, was critical for a woman; after Alison's parents divorced, her mother's job gave her a sense of power and control over her life that she otherwise would not have had. Now that Alison was an adult, her mother had a way of cutting through the superfluous to help her make decisions. Do not tolerate this, Shirley told her oldest daughter, echoing Bill's advice.

What should I do here? Alison asked Michelle Friedman, a psychiatrist and one of her closest friends since they'd attended college together and then medical school at New York University. Friedman's first impulse was to take dramatic action. She believed academic medicine, with its tiers of entrenched hierarchy, was rife with sexist attitudes that needed to be challenged. Call CBS. Call *The New York Times*. But the suggestions all involved a degree of jeopardy, and Friedman calmed down, aware her suggestions could seriously damage Alison's position at the hospital, if not ruin it. She knew Alison had worked too hard to want to destroy what she had built. Friedman recommended that Alison approach the chairman of the surgery department and have it out with him in a cool and controlled way.

After Friedman hung up the phone, she realized that she had just heard Alison's self-assurance falter for the first time, and it disturbed her. She'd never met anyone quite like Alison, a child of privilege raised on Fifth Avenue and 96th Street, and ever since they'd been friends Friedman had been impressed with Alison's seemingly boundless confidence. Anything seemed to be possible from Alison's perspective, and that belief had always

been immensely attractive to Friedman, the child of
Holocaust survivors, raised on a farm in the Catskills,
and a perpetual worrier. Friedman even thought that
part of surgery's allure for Alison had been its reputation
as the most macho and toughest of all medical fields; Alison was the only woman in their medical class to choose
it. She and Alison had talked about it then, but Alison
had discounted the image as a bad public-relations problem, unsupported by her own experience. She might
have to endure crude jokes—maybe—in the locker room,
but nothing more, she told Friedman. Neither she nor
Friedman had anticipated financial inequity, certainly
not at a supposedly enlightened Ivy League institution
like Columbia, in New York of all places.

Keith Reemstma, the chairman of the department of
surgery, was a tall, slender man with white hair and
glasses and a congenial, unhurried deameanor that reminded Alison of a popular town minister. Reemstma,
who had been a resident at Columbia 30 years ago and
returned in 1971 to become chairman, had an office on
the 14th floor of the hospital's aging administrative
building and he often liked to muse for a few minutes
about its commanding view of the Hudson River and
Manhattan. But Alison was in no mood for chitchat
when they met a couple of days later. "How else can this
be interpreted but as chauvinism?" she demanded. "We
are doing the same thing. We came in at the same time,"
she stated.

Reemstma seemed to measure his words before
speaking. She was not being paid less because she was a

woman, Alison later recalled Reemstma saying. It was an oversight. Besides, he hadn't known if she was going to work out. He assured her that the hospital would equalize the salary.

Alison was not giving up quite so easily. The hospital, she suggested, owed her $80,000 to even out the compensation—$40,000 for the first year and $40,000 for the current one.

"It's water under the bridge," he demurred, ushering her out of the office. Though Alison had never been told this and their opinions of her since had changed, he and his deputy initially had set her salary lower because they had viewed Alison as a temporary hire.

Alison could be confrontational, but if she was rebuffed, especially by someone in a position of authority, she tended to back off. She knew she was a weak negotiator, cowardly, in fact, when it came to talking about money. Besides, why allow a nonmedical question to spoil a job she loved? She'd amassed an unusual amount of responsibilty for a surgeon in her mid-thirties, she told herself. She already ran the breast clinic, the hospital's facility for poor women, and was beginning to run the tumor board meetings, the weekly discussions of current cases. She began telling herself that the salary differential was a minor irritant.

When Friedman later inquired about the outcome, Alison replied, "It's water under the bridge," unconsciously adopting Reemstma's phrase. Alison had a habit of finding something she liked in virtually every situation, and Friedman knew Alison wanted Columbia to work for her. Alison could push only so far without making life miserable for herself. Still, Friedman couldn't help thinking that the difference in pay had made Alison feel unrespected and devalued. Was she being paid less because they thought less of her?

Alison later raised the salary gap with the department's new business manager, who had not been on staff when she was hired. After reviewing the salaries, he told her he found the discrepancy unfair and inconsistent. Although all salaries were negotiated individually at Columbia and the hospital was under no obligation to offer an employee more than he or she said she was willing to accept, he agreed the figures did not look good even if the men had said they wouldn't accept less than $100,000 while Alison had been delighted to accept the first offer. He promised to urge for an adjustment. (Though he didn't mention it, he'd even found a third male surgeon hired at the same time who was earning more, but he was a cardiac surgeon and cardiac surgeons typically earn more than general surgeons.)

By the end of the year, Alison earned $88,000. The following year she made almost $92,000, and in 1988 she finally topped $100,000 to make $110,000.

Alison hadn't intended to specialize in breast surgery, and even had resisted when she had received a letter shortly after being asked to join the staff, informing her that she was expected to concentrate on breast surgery. "I'm not trained to do this. I'm trained in general surgery," she had told Paul LoGerfo, the head of general surgery at the hospital and Reemstma's deputy. Breast operations were considered a lower form of surgery because the procedure itself was not complicated and did not involve vital organs, making it less life-threatening than other surgeries and therefore less appealing to most surgeons. But LoGerfo had waived off her protests. "You have to find a niche in this world," he said then, and hers very well could be with the breast service. The two senior surgeons in that division were nearing retirement, and their departure would create a rare opportunity in an old institution like Columbia, where procedures and personnel changed slowly. A naturally enthusiastic man, LoGerfo was warming to his task of describing the benefits to her and the hospital. Although the breast service was extremely busy, he did not need to remind her that as an entity it was a mess, run more like a private practice than as a forum meeting its responsibility as part of a teaching hospital to instruct people about the disease. It needed to be taken in a new direction, and if anyone could take advantage of the opportunity to make it a vibrant part of the hospital it was she.

When Alison continued to object, a colleague became blunt. A female surgeon would have more difficulty attracting male patients than a male surgeon would. Men don't want to see women doctors, and they certainly don't want to see women surgeons.

LoGerfo had always looked out for Alison, and Alison considered him a mentor. She trusted him not to steer her wrong. Besides, it was apparent that the choice was not really hers if she wanted to stay at Columbia.

Even though she had not wanted to do it, Alison had quickly realized that LoGerfo was right: the breast service was a good niche for her. She was a naturally compassionate person, and more social than most surgeons, who as a group tended to keep a distance from their patients. Breast-cancer patients needed an enormous amount of counseling and support, and unlike other surgical patients, who usually accepted the surgeon's advice with comparatively few questions, they had tremendous angst about how their bodies would look and usually wanted to talk everything out. What kind of bras could they wear? Could they go swimming? Should they have a mastectomy or a lumpectomy? The relationship was intensely personal and intensely individualized, factors that appealed to Alison.

She'd also been given a lot of leeway by the two senior breast surgeons in the service, who willingly had turned large chunks of responsibility over to her. When she discovered that residents knew almost nothing about reading mammograms or the biology of breast cancer, even as they performed lumpectomies and mastectomies, she had made it her job to spend a portion of each operation instructing the residents on the science of breast disease, and directed the two other surgeons in the division to do likewise. Under her leadership, the tumor board meetings had been transformed from poorly structured monthly gatherings attended by one or two doctors to lively weekly sessions, pulsing with information and crowded with surgeons and other doctors involved with the care of breast-cancer patients. Both senior breast surgeons repeatedly assured her it was only a matter of time before she took over the helm. Sven Kister, a sweet native of Estonia, regularly promised her that she would inherit his practice once he retired. Frank Gump, the other senior breast surgeon and the chief of the service, had made an even more explicit promise. "Don't worry, Alison, you'll inherit all of this because I'm just getting to the end of the line here," he told her early one morning, after wearily glancing at the huge stack of mammograms they were meeting to examine in the office of the mammographer, Thane Asch. Gump was one of the busiest breast surgeons in New York City, and working seven days a week, often until nine at night. He couldn't take it any longer. His patients were sucking him dry. They needed so much reassurance. It was all getting to be too much. Asch, who had met with Gump nearly every morning at 6 for more than 20 years, had heard it all before. Gump told him all the time that Alison was going to take over the breast service.

Midway through 1990, Gump 62, announced that he planned to retire at the end of the year. It was clear that Kister, who was ailing, was not going to take over. "I am the new chief of the breast service," Alison, now 38, announced to Bill when she arrived home that Friday night. "This is going to be really great." Being the chief did not mean earning a lot more money, which she did not need—she'd already built up her practice rapidly and was making around $200,000 a year—but the title gave her the power to start new programs, conduct more research—make all the decisions, in other words, without first checking with someone else. "I can do things my way," she said. Her mother had died in a plane crash the previous fall, and this was the first really good news she'd had in a year. Alison actively began making plans, and one of the first items on her list was to hire another surgeon for the breast service. She wanted a woman because she was beginning to feel isolated and wanted to work with someone more like herself. Through colleagues she found Freya Schnabel, then a 32-year-old surgeon at Downstate Medical Center in

Brooklyn, whom she began to actively recruit.

Kister retired in August and Alison assumed the transition was beginning. But not long after his departure, Alison was walking down a hospital hallway when she ran into Gordon Schwartz, a well-respected breast surgeon from Philadelphia. Her face lit up on seeing her old friend. It was a Tuesday. "What are you doing here?" she asked. "I'm here to take over Frank Gump's job," he replied. Alison could feel her stomach sink. She numbly took a few steps alongside him. Schwartz was heading toward Reemstma's office. Alison's breath quickened. She could not believe she had been so naïve—again.

The next morning, Alison stormed into Reemstma's office. This time she was not going to be compliant. That was money; this was work. "I've been told all along that I was going to be the head of the breast service," she said. Alison clipped her words when she was mad, almost as if she were biting them. Columbia rarely hired outside of its staff for its supervisory positions. Why had she not been told about this? Reemstma said Schwartz's name had only come up Friday.

"I have a home number," she said sharply.

It was an oversight, Reemstma responded. Alison noticed these were the same words he had used to explain away her salary discrepancy. Reemstma explained that one of the hospital's senior doctors, David Habif, had recommended Schwartz because, with Kister and Gump departing, the hospital needed an additional doctor performing breast surgery. Schwartz was "really great," one of the big names in breast surgery, and, having been a resident there, was already part of the "Columbia family." Gump, he added, also had suggested Schwartz as his replacement. Alison could barely process his words she was so angry. All along they had been telling her, "You're doing a great job."

Reemstma tried to calm her, pointing out that she was only 38 years old while Schwartz was 55. He would retire soon. Exasperation was beginning to creep into his voice. Gump and Kister had attracted a huge number of patients, making Columbia the second biggest breast service in the city. Schwartz had a large practice and could bring a lot of patients with him. "Your practice is only half his size," he pointed out. "That's not enough." Left unsaid was what almost everyone at the hospital knew: Columbia, an inner-city hospital used by many patients with no insurance at all, was in dire financial straits, with annual losses of about $30 million a year. The breast service drew in a lot of money because the patient volume was so much larger than it was in other kinds of surgeries. While a person referred by a cardiologist to a cardiac surgery inevitably needed surgery, the majority of breast patients who have lumps do not. Most of the breast patients were insured.

Perhaps Alison and the Pennsylvania surgeon could be cochiefs, he suggested.

The proposal immediately struck Alison as ridiculous and unworkable. She knew Schwartz. He had just received a master's degree in business administration in addition to his medical degrees. "He is not going to be cohead of anything," she said.

Even though Schwartz had a bigger practice and more years, she felt that his academic credentials were no better than her own. By this time she had authored or co-authored 26 papers.

Alison next confronted Gump. She reminded him of his promises, which he dismissed as irrelevant in the context of the current situation. Two giant practices were going down the tubes, and Columbia needed more volume than Alison could bring in on her own. When he had told her she would be chief he had had no idea Kister was going to leave, too. She was too young to do it by herself.

In her mind, she translated his remarks: "You're basically only a woman and we need one of these gray-haired old men in here."

Alison left the office and called Jennifer Patterson, one of her closest friends of ten years and a dermatologist. Patterson had recently left New York University to start up her own practice because she had become fed up with the pettiness of academic medicine. She had come to the conclusion that a female doctor was only better off in an academic institution if she was single or divorced with children and a mortgage to pay, not married as she was, and especially not married to a wealthy man. She was convinced she had been denied raises because her superiors thought her husband, Howard Stringer, who was president of the CBS network and made a huge salary, could provide for her. Listening to Alison infuriated Patterson all over again, but she knew that mere anger was not what Alison needed at the moment. She summoned Stringer to the phone. He was calmer than she was and would offer Alison straight advice, untainted by emotion. He gave her the name and phone number of a labor lawyer.

Alison spoke to the lawyer. "This is very bad," the lawyer said. She ticked off the advantages Alison had in a sexual-discrimination lawsuit: Alison was the only female general surgeon at Columbia, she had been paid 60 percent of her two male colleagues' salaries and she was now being passed over. But, the lawyer cautioned, there were also major drawbacks to filing a lawsuit, and Alison would have to weigh them carefully. "You may create enemies of the people you work with," she warned. "You may have to leave."

Alison mulled over her options for a couple of weeks before deciding not to risk a lawsuit. Patterson didn't disagree with her decision. If Alison had taken action, others at the hospital probably would say it was a very poor show to sue, even if she was right, she told Alison. Patterson also privately wondered what else Alison had in her life at the moment. Her mother was dead. She did not have kids. Surgery, her work, was the center of her life, more primary even than her marriage. Surgery was her one certainty.

In the end, Alison's decision was rendered moot: Columbia's efforts to hire Schwartz fizzled. Reemstma apologized to Alison for his handling of the incident. "Great. Now I'm chief," she said, her voice reflecting a mixture of self-confidence and nervousness.

"No," Reemstma paused, "we still need to get more people up here." The hospital was going to try to recruit David Kinne, the head of the breast cancer center at the famed Memorial–Sloan Kettering Cancer Center, and Columbia's rival hospital. Kinne was the best-known breast surgeon in the country, and the idea of working with him actually appealed to Alison. "This is a nationally prominent guy. We're all going to learn something from him," she told Freya Schnabel, who had joined the staff in December.

Kinne, in time, also rejected Columbia's offer, and LoGerfo, the head of general surgery, called Alison into his office. He'd persuaded Reemstma, he said, to make her the chief of the breast service. Alison, however, did not feel that she had scored much of a triumph. It was appointment by default, and Reemstma's endorsement wasn't exactly unqualified. In fact, it sounded tentative.

Over dinner one night, Alison described her tenuous position to an aunt of Bill's, a former garment-industry executive, who had risen to the presidency of her company after a fierce struggle. "You just have to be smarter than these guys and work like a dog," his aunt counseled. The only way Alison was going to get what she wanted was to do it herself, she said. No one was going to hand it to her. "You have to be really up front. You can't shirk away," she said. "You just get a plaque made up and put it on the door and let the world know this is what you are." Send out a memo with the same information. Make up new business cards. "Publicize yourself, and it will be accepted eventually," she insisted, sensing that Alison was afraid and insecure. "You've got to be aggressive. That's the way a man would do it."

Nobody at Columbia flashed his or her title except the chairmen. On the other hand, Alison asked herself, what did she have to lose? Almost six months had passed since Gump had retired. Alison sat down at her desk at home and started composing a pamphlet to send out to the 3,000 or so doctors affiliated with Columbia, listing the names, phone numbers, titles, and services available at the breast service. At the top was Alison Estabrook, M.D., Chief, Breast Service. Alison nervously carried the finished memo to Reemstma's office. There was no way she would send it out without his approval. That would be too audacious. With LoGerfo standing at her side, Reemstma scanned the memo and told her to go ahead and send it.

Emboldened, she next ordered an office door sign from the hospital workshop. She had new business cards made up.

Several weeks later, Paul LoGerfo pulled Alison aside. All hell was breaking loose. Reemstma, the chairman, was under pressure from two prominent and extremely well-connected doctors to remove her as the chief, LoGerfo said. The first, a male gynecologist, LoGerfo said, didn't like how she treated his patients and had complained to Reemstma that female patients who chose to go to male gynecologists preferred to go to male surgeons if they had lumps in their breasts. If they weren't seen by male surgeons they would take their business to other hospitals. Other male gynecologists had made similar arguments to Reemstma, but this one was the most vocal. LoGerfo suspected the gynecologist was worried that if he sent a woman patient to a woman surgeon the patient might discover she preferred a woman doctor, especially for something like gynecology, and not want to return to him. Because he treated a number of women who liked to be referred to the chief—the chief of neurology, the chief of whatever his patients wanted—LoGerfo surmised the gynecologist did not want to risk referring them to Alison. The other doctor protesting Alison's appointment, David Habif, was one of the hospital's most senior surgeons and her most powerful detractor. Habif, 77, had complained to Reemstma that Alison did not have the experience or national reputation to take over.

Under ordinary circumstances, the doctors' objections might not have been enough to force Reemstma's hand. The problem LoGerfo felt was that both doctors, particularly Habif, were close friends of Seymour Milstein, the chairman of the hospital's board of trustees and part of a triumvirate running the hospital. The Milstein Family Foundation was the hospital's largest donor and its largess was evident throughout the hospital. A new 745-bed state-of-the-art building with glass skywalks was named for the family after the foundation recently donated $25 million for its construction. Alison performed her operations there. The Milsteins had endowed a chair for Habif—the Morris and Rose Milstein Professor of Surgery—which he had held since 1972, and Habif was Seymour Milstein's family physician.

Milstein, LoGerfo said he was told, was opposed to her being the chief of breast service.

Alison could not believe what she was hearing. "Who the hell are they?" she demanded angrily. "What do they know about breast surgery?"

"The decision is totally biased," LoGerfo said, his own anger rising. "It is not fair and it is political." If the decision had been his to make, she would have been the top candidate from the start, even over Kinne, because she was hungry and had proven she was willing to do the work to turn the breast service into a real service, not just something for herself.

He'd tried arguing with Reemstma without success. LoGerfo did not believe Reemstma was now objecting to Alison on the basis of gender. That was the gynecologist's problem. He thought Reemstma was trying to be politically correct. Reemstma, in LoGerfo's view, was spineless, unwilling to challenge the people in power. He thought Reemstma and the other doctors deserved to get in trouble, and he urged her to complain to the dean of students. "You need to be totally aggressive about it," he said.

LoGerfo thought Alison should sue the hospital; he would even testify for her. He had had plenty of conversations about her with Reemstma and letters that could be used in a suit to back up a claim that the decision to remove her was political and economic rather than based on merit, he later told her.

LoGerfo also had confronted Habif about his complaints. When Habif told him that Alison did not know enough surgical technique, LoGerfo told him he was wrong and missing the point. Her technique was just different from his. "Alison knows surgical care very well," LoGerfo stressed. But trying to change Habif's opinion was like talking to a concrete wall. Habif belonged to the school of surgery that aimed for perfection. That meant aiming for literally no bleeding at all. But LoGerfo believed that such perfectionism could actually endanger a patient's recovery, since perfect surgery meant making a bigger hole, keeping the patient under anesthesia longer, spending more time in the operating room. Perfect meant more pain and more risk. Alison did not practice perfect; neither did he. In LoGerfo's mind that was to her credit, not her detriment. The bottom line in surgery should be focused on how the patient heals, not on the technique.

(Milstein said in a later interview that he had not opposed Alison's appointment. "I don't know the lady," he said. Although he wasn't suggesting that anyone in particular had done so in Alison's case, he cautioned that people often used his name without his knowledge at the hospital when they wanted to accomplish something. "People like to say this is what the chairman wants," he said, before adding that he could not imagine telling a doctor what to do with much success. "They're gods as far as we lay people are concerned," he said.)

Alison did not want to go outside the chain of command to complain, as LoGerfo suggested, and shortly after their conversation she approached Reemstma in his office. She could not understand why she shouldn't be chief if the two biggest names in breast surgery in the vicinity had turned down the hospital's offers. Breast surgery was a very small field and there were only a handful of surgeons at the top. When Reemstma said he couldn't do it, Alison mentioned LoGerfo's comments about Habif and the gynecologist. Still hoping to avoid a confrontation, she reminded the chairman that two male surgeons were affiliated with the breast service. Reemstma waved her off. One was too heavily involved in research and primarily performed thyroid surgery. He had some other complaint about the other male surgeon.

Alison pressed. This was ridiculous. There had to be something more to this. Reemstma looked exasperated. The hospital needed to continue to search. Alison brought enthusiasm, dedication and youth to the job. He thought she was a very good surgeon and had done a superb job of organizing the breast clinic. But he also believed he had a duty as the chairman to listen to Habif and the gynecologists. Habif was the senior surgeon at the hospital and a thoughtful, fair man in his view.

Pressure also was being exerted on him by the people running the hospital to find someone else with more national stature. He needed to see if anyone else might be available.

She was promised all these things, she said in desperation. But even as she spoke, she could not believe she was having this conversation. Nothing this terrible had happened to her in her thirteen years at the hospital.

If a doctor was a good doctor, patients would remain loyal, whether the doctor was a man or a woman. She herself had a male gynecologist. Alison left the office dejected.

Sitting on a metal chair in an office of the hospital's clinic for low-income women, Alison recounted her conversations with LoGerfo and Reemstma to Freya Schnabel. Although Schnabel had been working with Alison for less than a year, they had become each other's closest confidant at the hospital, and their strengths fit together like a lock and key. Alison was the insightful, sharp intellect with superior judgment and skill, but uncomfortable with public-speaking engagements; while Schnabel was the entertaining extrovert, interested in expanding the breast service to include community outreach programs. They were the only women in general surgery at the hospital, and bit by bit, they were strengthening each other, as well as the breast service.

Up until this point, Schnabel could not understand the hospital's reluctance to appoint Alison the permanent chief. Alison couldn't have been busier, and a number of the changes she had instituted were beginning to show results, making the service more cohesive and bringing it more in line with other modern cancer centers. This latest piece of information was like the missing piece in a puzzle; its appearance helped her see the full picture.

Schnabel told Alison she had heard that the gynecologist was also complaining about the quality of treatment of the breast service, and from enough different sources to make them troubling. "You really need to set this guy straight," she said, suggesting that Alison call the gynecologist. "If he has a problem he should talk with you. Don't put up with this garbage." Emboldened, Alison picked up the phone and asked for the gynecologist. She could tell he was startled.

"I've heard you have these complaints about the breast service. What are your complaints?" she asked curtly. Alison's voice rose. "You're spreading these rumors behind my back and I want to hear what you're saying."

At some point, the gynecologist reiterated the statement about women wanting to see male breast surgeons.

There were two male surgeons affiliated with the breast service. What was wrong with them, she demanded? When he repeated again that some women wanted to see male breast surgeons, Alison scribbled it down.

"I've had it," she said, her temper flaring. "This is completely chauvinistic and untrue." She ticked off the names of male gynecologists who regularly referred patients to her. "They have no problems. You've never referred anyone."

The gynecologist interrupted, telling her he thought

the conversation should end because she was becoming hysterical.

Aware that she had lost control of herself, Alison tried to regain her composure and asked that he direct future complaints to her before going to the chairman of the department. She hung up the receiver.

Alison felt stupid and sick to her stomach when she rested the phone in its cradle. What had she gotten herself into? she asked herself, worried about the repercussions. If he had been any other gynecologist she would not have cared, but his connections made him powerful.

Schnabel, who had overheard the conversation, was livid and incredulous that the gynecologist had repeated his assertion about women and male doctors. "It's bad enough for someone to say that behind your back, but it's worse that he would feel comfortable saying it to your face," she told Alison.

As she expected, Reemstma called. The gynecologist had called to complain about her call and said she had been "way out of line." Do not speak to him anymore about his complaints, Reemstma told her.

After a third male surgeon under consideration for the breast service was taken out of the running, Alison approached Reemstma to discuss the next step. She was determined not to be a pushover. Who else was there, anyway?

There was still pressure to find another candidate, Reemstma told her, but no one appeared to want to come. To satisfy everyone, he said, he had decided to set up a committee to examine the breast service and, ostensibly, to consider whether Alison should be retained or a new head should be appointed. It wouldn't be a big deal, or very formal, he said, and she could put some of her friends on the committee. Committees like this were formed all the time at Columbia and from his point of view, it could be a good thing for her. Committees not only helped select chiefs, but they also improved the life and work of the person who was appointed by showing that the person had the support of his or her colleagues. That, Reemstma believed, would be far more important to her than that the chairman had picked her.

Alison left the meeting feeling that Reemstma was trying to assure her not to worry. That it would come out in her favor. It wasn't exactly what Alison had in mind, but Alison told herself she was prepared to wait for the committee's findings if the delay meant she would be the chief in the end.

She couldn't help wondering, however, if she was fooling herself and hearing what she wanted to hear. LoGerfo certainly felt the committee would not do her any good, and he was continuing to urge her to take action. Maybe she should quit and transfer her practice to another hospital and take her patients with her, as her good friend Jennifer Patterson was encouraging her to do. Why should she go through these repeated humiliations? At the same time, Columbia's prestige, facilities, and superior staff were important to her. Why should she be driven out? she asked, giving herself a pep talk. The old chauvinists were all nearing retirement and would be gone soon. Then it would all change. Besides, how did she know if it would be better someplace else? There were no significant divisions headed by women in any of the hospitals she might consider.

Back when she was still a resident, Alison had been warned by a woman plastic surgeon on staff that her job would be tougher at Columbia because she was a woman. As she described her frustration at Columbia to Alison at a party, the woman had broken down in tears. At the time, Alison had thought too much alcohol had heightened the woman's emotions. The surgeon later left the hospital, followed by the few other remaining women surgeons, but at the time Alison had attributed their departures to personal rather than systemic problems. More recently, Alison had been following the resignation of a prominent female neurosurgeon from a different perspective. Dr. Frances K. Conley had stunned the medical community with her announcement that she was resigning from Stanford Medical School after enduring what she claimed was a quarter-century of subtle sexism there. Her resignation prompted a flood of articles about how academic medicine demeaned women. If someone like Conley couldn't make it, who could? Alison wondered. How could she? Only 4 percent of medical-school department heads and only 6 percent of the nation's 38,000 surgeons were women, and there seemed to be widespread agreement that surgery was still the staunchest of the male bastions.

Alison's female medical students reported that when they interviewed for residencies they were always asked about their plans for children; the men never were. The older men seemed to take it for granted that women doctors were not as committed as the men.

When she was in a good mood, Alison could appreciate the irony of her own decision not to have children, a choice she had made almost exclusively because of her career. She'd flirted briefly with the idea early in her marriage, and even tried in vitro fertilization after not conceiving despite not using birth control for some time. Bill had wanted children, and she did not want to disappoint him so she agreed to undergo the procedure. But she'd been relieved when it failed and never tried again. She couldn't see where she would find the time a child needed, and Bill hadn't seemed overly enthusiastic about the day-to-day logistics of caring for a child.

Unlike her friends who came fresh to the experience of motherhood and working, Alison knew from her own experience how a child might feel about a parent who was often unavailable. Her mother had worked all the time, and even though Alison could now empathize with her mother's need for a career, Alison still could not erase her childhood impression of her mother as cold and uninterested. Her father, a freelance cameraman with a large inheritance, was the fun-loving and involved one, who was willing to hang out with his children in the family's apartment. Her parents had eventually divorced when Alison was 13. She did not know any women surgeons who had worked it out satisfactorily. Her sister-in-law, a vascular surgeon, had round-the-clock help; still she had no time for herself or to write papers, even though she was extremely talented. Schnabel rose at 5:30 and left the house before her two children awoke and often returned home after they were asleep. Another good friend had cut back her practice to care for her two small children, and still she complained to Alison about her life. Alison was unwilling to cut back on her career, and the memories of her own childhood would tear her apart if she had a child.

Their schedules left even less time for a child now. Bill

commuted to his job as a neuropathologist at Yale University School of Medicine in New Haven, Connecticut and spent Tuesday and Thursday nights there. She saw 30 to 40 patients a day on Monday, Wednesday and Friday, and operated all day Tuesday and Thursday. By the time she arrived home, she was completely overloaded and exhausted.

The committee to determine her future began meeting in late 1991, and her allies on it included three doctors she saw daily: a pathologist (a woman), a radiation oncologist (a woman), and a mammographer. The committee also included a male surgeon, a female gynecologist, a male vice-president from the business side of the hospital, a medical oncologist, and a couple of other surgeons.

Although the deliberations were supposed to be confidential, a few of the committee members, as well as the witnesses, kept Alison informed about the proceedings as the committee met into the winter of early 1992. As she discovered, the committee was turning out to be more serious than she thought.

Thane Asch, the mammographer and one of her confidantes, had met with Alison almost daily since her arrival at the breast service. He thought she was extremely talented, as well as good with patients and efficient. He'd hoped for the longest time that she would be named the next chief. But it didn't take long for Asch, a wiry man in his 60s, to begin to think that, contrary to what Alison had told him, the committee had been put together to say she was unacceptable. Some of the strongest objections about her were coming from an administrative vice-president who was arguing the hospital needed to find someone with more pull than Alison. It seemed to Asch that he was speaking for the administration. Because Asch had announced his pending departure from the hospital, he thought that he could speak candidly without worrying about the ramifications of going against the administration, unlike his younger colleagues who still had to work there.

After David Habif, one of the two doctors whose opposition had led to her troubles, testified that Alison's surgical technique was not up to par, Asch launched into a long defense. He described how Alison always came back with the right specimen after he inserted a guide wire into a patient's breast to mark the spot where possible cancer cells had shown up on a mammogram but were not perceptible to touch. It was a difficult procedure that gave other surgeons trouble. "She comes back with the pathology every time," he later recalled saying. "She's better than the men," he added for emphasis, convinced the process was biased against Alison because of macho attitudes. Asch acknowledged that Alison's academic credentials were weaker than those of the two previous chiefs, who delivered lectures around the world, but she was much younger than they were and would develop. Asch's comments were met with little response, underlining his impression that his comments were not in line with the tone of the meetings. Although he thought Habif was a wonderful doctor, Asch believed he had too much influence in the hospital by virtue of his close association to the Milsteins.

Paul LoGerfo also testified strongly in Alison's favor. He said he would oppose appointing anyone other than Alison to head the breast service. She was doing a better job than anyone had ever done. Before Alison, he said, the service had been a joke. The breast service should be a forum for instruction, he said, and Alison was providing that. She might be a little immature, but when an institution sees someone going in the right direction, as Alison was, the institution should keep her and encourage her.

Asch agreed and he was becoming increasingly incensed. He thought it was unconscionable to tell her she was chief one day, allow her to make signs and pamphlets, and then the next month search for a new chief. He wanted off the committee. "I no longer want to serve," he announced one day. He told the committee it should disband and Alison be named the permanent chief.

Asch later reported to Alison that as far as he was concerned the committee had broken up without making a formal recommendation. He, at least, had not signed anything, nor had the committee members with whom he had conferred. The whole process was completely political, he said. There should be nothing to stop you from being accepted by the administration because there is nobody else to go after. Anyway, who would want to come up here under these circumstances? he asked.

Another committee member who supported Alison privately told her she was fighting the "old boy network" and should sue the hospital. Two other committee members, she was told, also had recommended terminating the search and naming her chief.

Frank Gump, the former chief of the breast service,

also had come around to believing that Alison deserved to be named the permanent chief. He conveyed his sentiments to Reemstma who contacted him from time to time to ask his opinion about various candidates for the job. "Look she's doing a good job. She should be chief," he said, citing her work at the breast clinic, her establishment of a registry of breast patients and the improvements she had made in the service's relationships with the medical oncologists. But Gump knew Alison faced a wall of resistance. Habif and the gynecologist were very influential, and the gynecologist had repeated his complaints to Gump about Alison's treatment of his patients and his belief that women wanted to see male surgeons. In Gump's opinion, the gynecologist gave his patients impeccable care, but he tended to be a chauvinist at times. Gump had heard there were members of the board of trustees who insisted the hospital could not appoint Alison, a young woman without a national reputation, as chief of the breast service after such a long history of big names at the helm. Milstein liked marquee names, in Gump's opinion, and Alison was not one of those. Milstein had been all over him not to leave.

Around the same time, *New York Magazine* listed Alison as one of the city's seven best breast surgeons in an article "The Best Doctors in New York"; to be included, a doctor had to be nominated by other doctors. She had received a congratulatory letter from Seymour Milstein. Two months later, in January 1992, Habif died.

Alison heard in March 1992 that a new committee was being formed, and that several new names of possible candidates had been suggested to the committee chairman. Paul LoGerfo had been removed as the head of general surgery, a move he attributed to his defense of Alison, though others said that was only part of the reason. He was replaced by Roman Nowygrod, a vascular surgeon. Tired and frustrated while waiting for others to act, Alison decided to set some deadlines to make decisions about her career. One benchmark would occur in July when she was up for an associate professorship at the medical school. If she did not make it she would have one more piece of information to evaluate the hospital's commitment to her.

In the meantime, she was working frantically to try to prove herself, seeing patients or operating 12 hours a day in an effort to show that not only was she as good a surgeon as anyone the hospital might find but that she also could bring in as much money. That would be the bottom line. She'd brought in nearly $1 million in patient billings in 10 months, one of the highest intakes in the entire department. Alison and Schnabel also had just started a well-received program for women at risk of developing breast cancer because of their family histories. The breast service was moving in the right direction, but the improvements seemed to have little effect on the hospital's continuing search for a permanent chief. She did not know how much longer she could put up with it, and the dribs and drabs of insults seemed to continue unabated.

Recently, a surgery resident in his last year of training had appeared in the doorway of her office and announced that he and the doctor overseeing the residents' training program had changed the operating procedures at the breast clinic. Fifth-year residents, he explained, would no longer help out with the surgery there. For years, fifth-year residents had performed the operations, assisted by second-year residents.

Breast surgery was easy and routine, he said, so from now on fourth-year residents would perform the operations with the second-year residents. Alison could barely control her fury. The decision was outrageous, she said. First, she pointed out, it was bad medicine. Second-year residents were just learning surgery. Assigning fourth-year residents to the breast clinic was a prescription for disaster. The fourth-year residents already were busy in the intensive care unit and might not get to meet a breast patient until the day of surgery. That was ridiculous. "It's not the way doctors are trained and it shouldn't be that way," she said.

Furthermore, Alison knew that the change in procedure meant she or another staff surgeon would have to be present at all future operations of clinic patients to make sure no errors were made.

Finally, Alison told the chief resident she was angry that he had not consulted her about the changes. "I am certainly surprised that I wasn't included in this as the chief of breast surgery," she told the resident.

In the face of her growing anger, the chief resident quickly backed off and said the change would not be made. But Alison made an appointment to see the doctor who oversaw the residents' program.

Once in his office, she repeated her complaints. After she finished, the doctor responded in a fatherly tone, "You don't want people to think that you're an angry woman do you, Alison?" he asked. Alison blinked rapidly. She hardly knew the man and saw him infrequently, usually less than once a month. She never saw him in the operating room. Alison did not bother to respond. This kind of stunt would never be pulled with the head of cardiac surgery. But she had made up her mind a while ago not to waste any more time trying to educate these guys. It was not worth it.

Still, after her meeting with the head of the residents' program, Alison spent days examining her behavior. She felt confused. She asked herself if maybe she was angry. Did she yell at the people who clean the floors? Did she yell at her secretaries? The people in mammography seemed to like her. She tried to be gracious to the operating-room staff and knew all their first names, unlike the male surgeons, who seemed to show their anger all the time. She certainly did not want to emulate them. She knew the female nurses particularly well because they used the same locker room to change into their operating uniforms, and she had checked many of their breasts. She was always being stopped in a hall by a nurse or someone else in the hospital to ask about their mammograms. People greeted her by name all the time. They did not run when she came into the room, as she had seen them do with some other surgeons.

But why had he said that? Maybe this was her reputation on the grapevine and she should take his admonition seriously. She asked Schnabel, who was always candid with her, whether she might be deceiving herself.

Schnabel told Alison to forget it, saying if a male surgeon had complained about the change of procedure no one would have suggested he was out of line. She'd seen male surgeons throw instruments in the operating room and act imperiously, without anybody's saying something. But if her tone varied from matter of fact, she was deemed hysterical. That was the universal perception of women surgeons. She tried to be calm even when she was deliberately provoked, but she told Alison there was nothing wrong with getting angry if the anger was justified. It was just one more trail she and Alison were going to have to forge as women in a field with very few.

Schnabel could see the search process was wearing on Alison, and placing her under unnecessary strain to achieve an unattainable goal. The hospital was looking for someone who did not exist: a big-name person who could bring patients with him. The only person in New York who could do that was David Kinne and he had turned them down. Large numbers of patients were not going to follow a surgeon from Baltimore or Pennsylvania. It was ridiculous to think they would.

Alison and I met in her office, a small, spare space on the sixth floor of the hospital's medical building, at the end of May 1992. The significance of the Milstein family to the hospital was immediately apparent. Signs everywhere, including one a short distance from her office, pointed to the Milstein Building Bridge, a glass-enclosed walkway leading to the large white office building named after the family. Alison's challenge appeared to be more daunting than I had suspected.

Alison's sign outside her own door still read: ALISON ESTABROOK, CHIEF OF BREAST SURGERY.

We had arranged to meet this day because Alison had said she was taking the week off. But when I arrived her receptionist directed me to the lounge not far from her office because she was running late. She was seeing patients.

Half an hour later, Alison hurriedly approached. She had on an emerald green dress and black patent-leather pumps. She had tied her hair back in a ponytail. She looked pale and exhausted and suggested we walk a few bleak blocks to a noisy bar and grill.

To prove herself over the last several months, she said, "I worked as hard as I could." Her billing had doubled. She looked nervously down at the table and then at me. She was worried she might be practicing bad medicine because she had too many patients and had to depend too much on nurses and other assistants to catch problems she might miss. She recently had decided not to accept any new patients, but even then, she said, the volume was crushing.

"As I see it, it's gotten way, way, way out of control, and I really don't feel like I know these patients, and I'm not too happy about this," she said, her voice picking up speed. "I feel like if I don't have backup from people that I normally count on, like nurses, I may miss something; like an anesthesiologist who told me, 'By the way, something's wrong with this cardiogram.' I wouldn't have seen it, and that's not good." She repeated herself. "It's not good. I don't like that."

About a third of the news she delivered to patients was bad, and she was bombarded with emotion all day long. It was not unusual for Alison to find a staff member crying, saying she could not tell a patient what the findings of a test were. Alison was worn down, physically and psychologically.

"You have to have a special temperament for this. It's a lot of talking, a lot of psychological stuff, a lot of holding of hands," she continued. "It's sort of weird because colon cancer's much, much worse than breast cancer, but when you tell somebody they have colon cancer they generally don't completely freak out. . . . But with breasts it's a big decision." She had to read the patients and guide them. "You spend a lot more time talking. It's very intense."

Friedman, her psychiatrist friend, had told Alison that she could not feel guilty about turning away patients. "You're not good if you're burnt out, exhausted, and re-sentful," Friedman had told her. "How many times can you tell a 27-year-old she has cancer and is going to die and see your secretaries weep into their typewriters?" Friedman had asked.

Alison did not disagree in theory. "But the fact of the matter is that it's very hard, because there are hysterical women calling on the phone all the time, and the secre-taries can't handle all of this. They just can't do it. It's just hard. It's different from dealing with a skin thing and 'I can see you tomorrow or next week,' " Alison said. I could see she was wound up.

Alison did not need prompting to continue. "I don't really want to do this. I can't do this anymore. I am com-pletely frazzled. I need to slow down. I feel like I'm not in control."

She had wanted to prove to the committee that she was as good as anyone, but she was not sure if it was worth it. "I sometimes think, 'Well, why am I doing this? Why am I doing this?' This is driving me crazy. Do I re-ally need this ego gratification to be the head of the breast service and bring in all this money to Columbia just to show these people that I can do it? What is the point of this? And, so now, I'm really actively deciding

I'm not going to bring in all this money to Columbia. I'm not going to see all these new patients. I'm going to calm down now. It's gotten way, way out of hand, and it's just too much and I've got to stop doing this."

But controlling her schedule had turned out to be harder than she expected. She typed statements for her secretaries to read to new patients seeking an examination.

"I tell my secretaries, 'read this little thing that says Dr. Estabrook is not seeing any new patients. And you will have to see her associate, Dr. Schnabel.' I have to tell them what to say, otherwise I always get talked into these things. But they still leave me messages," she said with exasperation.

For example, that day her secretary told her she had to immediately call a doctor who was hysterical because his wife had an abnormal mammogram. "So I said, 'What happened to your little typed card: "Dr. Estabrook is not seeing any new patients"?' You just read that. And she said, 'I couldn't do it. He was hysterical. He works here. I know his baby-sitter. You've got to see the wife.' I said, 'No, I'm not. I'm not going to do it. I'm not going to do it.' I didn't. She's going to see Freya tomorrow. But sometimes it doesn't work."

As we spoke, Alison attempted to ignore the beeper that had sounded several times from somewhere inside her pocket. It was after 7 P.M., dinnertime, and she supposedly was on vacation. When it buzzed one more time she pulled out the small black box and read the message on the tiny screen. A patient wanted to reschedule the next day's surgery because her mother had died. I asked if she wanted to return the call. No, she said. We would return to the office later, and she would call the woman.

She said she had even thought about taking a leave of absence from the hospital. "Which has never been done," she pointed out. "I mean surgeons never do it. I think I could be the first one to do it and not be pregnant and just say, Look, I'm taking two months off and I'm going to Cambodia or somewhere."

I asked whether she liked having the extra money. After expenses she had cleared about $500,000 in the past 11 months.

"It's not worth it. It's not worth it," she repeated. "I have to come to a decision here about what is my overall plan in life. One of my friends told me that she thought about that when she was 40 years old: What was her overall plan, how many more years was she going to work, what was she going to do? And I thought, God, you know, I just play this thing day by day. I don't really think about this as overall plans of what I'm going to be doing ten years from now. But I think I'm going to have to start thinking about this."

The same friend, she said, had urged her to forget about pursuing the breast service. "Forget about this chief of breast service thing. What do you care?" her friend asked. Jennifer Patterson told her she had to be more adamant about not taking more patients. "You've got to just tell these people no and no and no," she told her. "You've got to get more control over this."

Her women friends played a central role in her life. She often had dinner with Michelle or Jennifer on the Tuesday and Thursday nights Bill was out of town, and she rarely took an important step or dealt with a problem without seeking their advice. They were her panel of experts to help her make decisions. But they hewed to more traditional gender roles, even if they had broken barriers by becoming doctors. Jennifer's life was intimately tied up with that of her husband, the president of CBS, and she wanted to have a child.

"I just had dinner with her last night, and she said her practice of dermatology is not her whole life by any means. And she's so involved in Howard's life and socializing and going out to her house and her garden and all those things that she makes her own hours. And she's not all that busy. Dermatologists are just not that busy."

Alison wanted to return to a more manageable caseload, but at the same time she worried that if she turned down too many new patients women would begin seeking treatment outside of Columbia, which would not look good for her. Her secretary kept tabs on what these women did. About half took her recommendation to see Schnabel, and the other half sought treatment elsewhere. She did not want hospital administrators to think she was turning away business—or money. It was a treadmill.

She was, however, taking other steps to cut back. CBS *This Morning* had called on Friday to interview her, but she recommended they speak with Schnabel. It was exactly what Schnabel needed to improve her standing—a spotlight that Alison thought could only alleviate some of her own pressure. Alison's father and her husband, however, had been furious with her for turning CBS down. Her father called and said she was insane to pass up an opportunity like that. Her husband argued her appearance would have shown the hospital she was respected in the field. A few months earlier, she might have agreed, but now she was too tired to worry about it. What was appearing on CBS anyway? It was not like getting the Nobel Prize, and it had nothing to do with her medical or academic life. She certainly did not need the publicity. She at least knew who she was or was becoming. Or perhaps exhaustion had triumphed over ambition.

The search for a new chief had been going on for over a year, and the hospital was currently considering another candidate, a surgeon from Florida. A surgeon from Ohio also had been temporarily considered.

The only bright spot for Alison was that the latest candidate had said he did not want to be limited to breast surgery and would consider coming to Columbia only if he could oversee all cancer surgery, a newly created position.

Nowygrod, the new head of general surgery, who at 45 was only five years older than she, had made a point of assuring her that she would keep her title as chief of the unit if the hospital could work out an arrangement with the Florida surgeon. The Florida surgeon would help her out, not supplant her.

"He would basically just help me and be like a friend and at the same level as I am," she said she was told. "He'll just be an ally, essentially." The Florida surgeon, a man in his early forties, had repeated his reassurances to her at a lunch about a month earlier. Alison, however, reserved judgment. The year and the endless, absurd process had taken its toll.

"This guy may say, 'Look I don't want to come to Columbia,' so then the whole search will be on again. So I don't really know." She paused, recalling the broken promises that had been made to her. "And they also do lie."

Alison's beeper went off again, and she thought she should head back to the office and then home. It looked as if I would not make the last flight back to Washington, so Alison invited me to spend the night at their house in Englewood. She called Bill and told him she was running late. It was after eight and they had instituted a rule that they both had to be home by eight on the nights they stayed together as a self-check against their tendencies to work late.

We first stopped back at her office. Her two secretaries were still there; one was trying to get a little ahead so she could take off some time the next day to attend a function at her son's school. The relationship between the three women seemed pleasant and casual. Alison's diplomas hung on the wall, and a row of small photographs rested on a bookshelf, including one of her in her white wedding dress in the garden with Bill.

When we arrived at her house about twenty minutes later Bill was standing at the stove, sautéing some beef. After a quick exchange of pleasantries, Bill told her about a phone call he had just received from a friend about a young relative who was in critical condition after suffering a brain aneurysm. The friend was worried the doctors treating the child were not doing enough. After describing the treatment, Bill asked Alison what she thought. She had her doubts about the quality, too, she said, but she cautioned he had to be very careful about giving advice in grim situations like this one, when the likelihood of death was great even with good care. "You make the parents feel guilty," she said.

Alison took me on a quick tour of the house. It had the look of a furnishing job never fully finished. Despite the lack of furniture in the living room and no curtains, the house had a warm, rich feeling. Several photographs hung on the wall, including a series of Janis Joplin nude taken by Annie Leibovitz, a friend of Alison's since they both were teenagers. Family photographs hung on other walls. Alison looked remarkably youthful.

When she saw me peering at one photograph, she said one patient recently told her she must be a very good doctor. "Why?" Alison said she asked.

"Because I saw you two years ago and now you look ten years older," the patient had said. "You must work very hard."

I set the alarm for six the next morning because Alison said she needed to make it to her office by 8:15. She had surgeries planned.

As we drove that morning, I asked her to explain why she referred to this week as her vacation. She said she had taken off the entire day on Monday and was taking off the next day, Friday, to travel with her husband to Block Island, off Rhode Island, where they planned to build a house. She referred to the other three days as vacation because she had used them to catch up on her backlog, seeing and operating on patients she had not been able to fit in earlier. She had not scheduled her weekly 7:30 breast-surgery meeting with her colleagues this morning.

On her schedule she had a biopsy of a young woman with a heart problem and a mastectomy on a woman doctor she had known since she was a resident. The doctor was 39 and in her first trimester of a long-awaited pregnancy. She had undergone an operation in January to improve her chances of becoming pregnant and had conceived in February. Alison had performed a biopsy on a suspicious lump on Friday that had turned out to be cancerous. The woman had not decided what to do about the baby. If she did not abort, her chances of dying increased because they could not treat her with chemotherapy while she was pregnant. Her husband wanted her to abort, but the woman was unsure.

Alison sounded pained by the woman's case. But I could also note that the level of edginess, the tension I heard in her voice when she discussed her career problems, had disappeared. Her speech even slowed. I mentioned this. "I am good at this," she said, dropping me off at the corner to catch a cab.

I later had a chance to judge for myself when Alison invited me to spend a day with her in the operating room. It was a Thursday and she had five surgeries scheduled: two mastectomies; two lumpectomies, in which only the tumor, not the whole breast, is removed; and a dissection of the lymph nodes.

Alison waved to me from the far corner of the cavernous hospital lobby. She was wearing light blue surgical pants, a short-sleeved top, and navy blue clogs. It was 9:15. She had been working since 7:30.

Her first mastectomy patient, a young woman in her early 30s in the second most severe stage of breast cancer, lay unconscious on the operating table. About ten people swarmed around her body, inserting intravenous needles and reading monitors and drawing incision lines. The woman wanted a new breast to take the place of the one removed, and a second team of surgeons was scheduled to operate simultaneously, crafting the new breast out of fat from the woman's abdomen. That portion of the surgery was expected to last ten hours, and both the plastic-surgery team and the anesthesiologist had brought a boom box to listen to music.

Alison carefully surveyed the preparations and, satisfied, announced the start of the operation. It was 9:45. She made an initial slice, then pierced the woman's skin with a hook that resembled a bicycle spoke. Alison lifted the skin, demonstrating to the two residents and the medical student on her team how to hold the skin open to expose the interior of the breast.

Alison continued to cut through the fatty tissue with a cauterizing knife that sealed the bleeding blood vessels at the same time. The woman had undergone months of chemotherapy to shrink the cancerous tumor, and Alison was concerned about blood loss because the woman's white-blood-cell count was very low. "We have to be very careful," she cautioned.

I had never witnessed an operation and was struck by a mastectomy's resemblance to something so methodical and impersonal as cutting fat from a chicken breast. A large oval-shaped incision was cut a few inches lower by the plastic surgeons and seemingly exposed what seemed like most of her interior. Alison interrupted the mood, telling the assembled group how much she liked the woman. "The man who comes with her is not her husband but he is very nice," she said. The descriptive digression was brief but humanizing, providing the natural transition to Alison's queries about the plans of the residents and the medical student.

The medical student, a woman, told Alison that a top administrator advised her to train as a surgeon if she wanted to have a family. He said she could plan her surgeries around her family schedule.

"You can't do that," Alison responded in disbelief. Part time would not work because surgeons needed to make rounds at the end of the day to check their patients and call family members. Patients did not want to wait to schedule their operations around the surgeon's schedule. They would go elsewhere. "Radiology is more a 9-to-5 job," Alison said.

At 10:40 Alison was finished with the mastectomy. Before moving on to her next patient, Alison and I took the elevator to see Thane Asch, the mammographer, who had prepared her next patient, a woman in her 40s. Tiny grains had showed up on the woman's mammogram that would be undetectable by touch, and Asch had inserted a wire in the area he thought Alison should remove.

"The breast is like concrete," Asch warned. "Make sure to scrape out a large section," he said, highlighting the spot on the mammogram for the lumpectomy. If the grains did not show up in an X-ray of the removed section, she would have to repeat the surgery.

"It will be torture for everyone," she said apprehensively.

A blue cloth screen had been raised between her head and body, shielding her from the operation. But Alison also was vigilant about any stray comments the residents might make. The woman, in her late 40s, had been administered a local anesthesia and would be conscious throughout the procedure. "They could say something like 'She has very bad cancer,'" Alison said just before we entered the room.

Alison greeted the woman warmly and told her if she felt any discomfort to speak up and more painkiller would be administered. Alison continued to talk to the woman as she cut through her skin and blood flooded the area under the nipple. "I need a lot of clamps and a lot of sponges," Alison told the young operating-room nurse standing at the end of the operating table. Her voice was calm, but the resident assisting her quickly began cauterizing the bleeding veins and sponging away blood. The nurse, however, was responding slowly. "Right now," Alison said firmly without raising her voice. When the patient moaned, Alison motioned for a syringe.

Alison cut loose the last attached area surrounding the wire and lifted it out of the woman's breast, squeezing what appeared to be a hard spot, and then deposited it in a container.

The container in hand, Alison walked briskly to the mammographer's office. She had discovered an unexpected mass and wanted the mammographer to X-ray it to make sure it contained the grains that showed up on the mammogram. "It wasn't there a couple of weeks ago," the mammographer said.

Alison then walked the sample over to the pathology lab, where the three pathologists fingered the mass. "It looks cancerous," one said, gesturing for Alison to examine a section under the microscope. Alison had recently operated on his sister-in-law for breast cancer. Alison peered through the lens, and her shoulders slumped.

"I hate this. I dread this," she said as we took the stairs to the operating room. She usually could tell in advance of surgery whether a lump was cancerous, giving her time to prepare her patient for bad news. But this time her instincts had been wrong.

The patient had not yet been moved to the recovery room, where Alison and the patient could talk privately. For the first time in my presence, she snapped. "This happens every day and it backs up the operating." After telling the still groggy patient that she was waiting for the results, Alison pulled out a pen with a wildly printed case. "A patient gave it to me. She said it would make me feel better every time I had to write down this diagnosis," she whispered, writing "microcal cancer" on the woman's chart.

Alison left the room and returned to the pathology lab, where the diagnosis was confirmed. "Wall-to-wall cancer," the pathologist said.

Alison could stall no longer. Her second patient had been moved to the recovery room. I could see Alison taking a deep breath as she pulled the yellow curtain around the bed for privacy. Alison said they had found a mass. It was cancerous.

"Why didn't it show up on the mammogram?" the woman asked, her voice trembling. Alison explained that there is always at least a 10 percent chance of a false reading. What if there was something in her other breast that did not show up on the mammogram? she asked, repeating a common fear of breast-cancer patients.

Alison patiently explained that her prognosis was good. The cancer had been discovered early. There would be follow-up surgery to examine her lymph nodes, and radiation therapy, which Alison could arrange at a hospital closer to her home. The woman, however, said she wanted to return to Columbia.

"She will probably not remember a word of what I said except that the news was bad," Alison said to me after emerging from behind the curtain. The woman was still sedated.

Alison's next stop was the waiting room to speak with the woman's brother and sister-in-law. "I hate this," she said again.

It was easy to pick them out in the waiting room. They were sitting at the edge of their seats, smiling anxiously at Alison's approach. She came straight to the point. "The prognosis is good, but she needs more surgery," Alison told the brother, whose eyes began to well up at the news.

Alison's next operation, a lumpectomy, went smoothly and quickly. Her patients were beginning to back up and she went straight to her next patient, a 58-year-old Medicaid patient who needed a mastectomy. Under normal circumstances the woman would have been treated at the breast clinic for low-income patients, but Alison had known the woman for a long time because she had performed a lumpectomy on her other breast.

As Alison began her incision, she told the residents that the woman wanted another lumpectomy, but she was not a good candidate. Why was that? Alison asked. Alison believed it was part of her job to make sure that the residents understood not only the surgical procedure but the science. She asked the residents if the new cancer was a recurrence from the old cancer? "It can't be a recurrence," one resident answered. Alison nodded and asked for an explanation.

Throughout the procedure she continuously pointed out the nerves, pale and almost indistinguishable from the tissue. Pinching one nerve, she showed how it made the muscle jump. "You must be extremely careful not to cut them or the arm will flap," leaving the patient with slightly impaired arm movement, she cautioned. It would be easy to cut one. At 3:15, Alison deposited the breast in a large paper bucket.

With one surgery left to go, Alison looked at her watch. Lunch at the hospital cafeteria was out of the question because it had long since closed. We stopped at her office and grabbed a drink and a yogurt from the small refrigerator in her office. At 4:20, Alison began the final operation of the day, on the wife of a doctor who needed to have her lymph nodes removed to see if her cancer had spread. If it had, that meant the cancer was moving through the body.

During the next two hours, Alison caught the end of the tumor board meeting and then checked on her patients still in the hospital, made calls to the hospital's employment office to straighten out a personnel matter, met with a medical student about a research project Alison was supervising, called the boyfriend of her first patient of the day, and spoke to a lawyer who wanted her to testify against another doctor in a medical malpractice case. It would anger her colleagues, but she thought she might if the doctor had been sloppy.

At 7:30, more than 12 hours after she had arrived at the hospital, Alison walked with me to the street outside the hospital. Her husband expected her home at 8 P.M. but she had a few more phone calls to make. I was tired. She looked the same as she had in the morning, except she had changed into a dress. She had 38 patients on her schedule for the next day.

In early summer of 1992, Reemstma and the chairman of the search committee met with Alison and told her they had decided to continue the search for a new chief who was more experienced and who had more name pull. The Florida surgeon had not yet made a decision, and another candidate, a doctor affiliated with a federal research institute, was arriving for interviews.

After meeting the candidate, Alison was infuriated. He was a year younger than she and was primarily a researcher. Alison protested to Nowygrod. The candidate had no publications in breast surgery. His specialty was sarcomas and melanomas. Besides, she felt his bedside manner was lacking. This had to be a joke. He looked so young Freya Schnabel started referring to him as Doogie Howser—the child doctor in the television series of the same name.

Alison once again was not sure how much longer she could put up with the snubs. Ever since the Philadelphia surgeon first arrived 18 months earlier to interview for the chief's job, she had felt her work and competence were being questioned without reason. She thought she possessed a strong sense of self, but the confidence and status others saw were beginning to seem like lies. She felt increasingly diminished. Maybe her well-practiced endurance had just allowed her to be pushed around. Nowygrod, who she had hoped would be an ally, was turning out to be no different from Reemstma. Why didn't her superiors recognize how great a job she was doing? Other than the political miscalculation of yelling at the complaining gynecologist, she felt she had made no other missteps, certainly no major ones. By any objective standard, she knew she had done a good job and her work was superior to that of a lot of other surgeons at Columbia. The department administrator had just told her she had billed more than anyone else in general surgery. She used to be able to rationalize her tolerance by saying she loved what she was doing. How much longer would that last?

She was still fuming when she received a phone call

near the end of June from the chairman of the surgery department at the University of California San Diego Medical Center. The hospital wanted to start a breast-surgery service, and she had been recommended to him. They were looking for a bright, energetic, intelligent woman to lead the breast division, he said. Was she interested?

Alison had a way out of Columbia. San Diego suddenly seemed like the greatest place in the world to live.

Bill was skeptical when she later told him about the call. "You'll never leave New York," he said, reminding her that she had hated California when she briefly attended the University of California at Berkeley as a freshman. After a year, she'd returned to New York to go to Barnard. They would have trouble selling their house. She knew he hated change and took his skepticism in stride. Alison told Reemstma she was considering the San Diego offer.

A few weeks later, on July 16, Nowygrod informed Alison that it was 75 percent certain that the doctor from the federal research institute was going to come to Columbia. His title would be Chief of Surgical Oncology/Breast, her division would be subsumed into his, and he would be her boss. "He tells me that I am perceived as a young, budding surgeon and that we need a stronger presence in breast," Alison wrote, recording her recollection of the conversation a few days later on her computer. "I was fairly shocked. I asked him why [he] couldn't be Chief of Surgical Oncology only. He isn't very interested in breast, and he wants to do sarcomas and melanomas and . . . breast."

Alison vented her anger when she ran into Nowygrod later in the hallway. She told him she was still very upset and reiterated her complaints about the candidate's qualifications. "He has none of my credentials," she said. "This reeks of chauvinism," she said, almost sputtering. "I would be happy to be under someone great in breast—like Kinne—but not someone less acomplished than I." Nowygrod told her that Columbia was falling down the tubes financially, and the hospital needed an oncologist, a cancer specialist, with national connections to get things moving. Alison could still run the breast service, he would just be above her in a newly created position as something like the "Associate Director."

Nowygrod thought his proposal was the best solution to what had become a mishandled personnel problem. Even though he thought Alison probably didn't trust anyone in the department anymore, he was an ally and determined to reassure her that he believed in her. He tried to explain that the position Associate Director would be a storefront title that would protect her and the department. But she had to understand reality. Reemstma was still under pressure from the administrative side of the hospital and some referring doctors—and these were some pretty powerful people who were close to some of the hospital trustees—to hire someone as chief of the breast service with a bigger name, more of a national reputation and more experience than Alison, and maybe even a male. At the same time, the hospital was looking for somebody to head up surgical oncology. By hiring somebody as the head of surgical oncology and administratively placing the breast service under it, he thought he could defuse the pressure and guarantee Alison the security of heading up the breast service.

His explanation did not appease her, and she appealed to his sense of fairness, reminding him he had daughters. They probably want to have careers, too. "Haven't you heard this is the year of the woman?" she said, referring to the spate of women candidates running for political office and one of the themes that had been highlighted that week at the Democratic National Convention, which had been held in the city. Even though Nowygrod was only a few years older than her, Alison thought he looked at her as if he didn't know what she was talking about.

"I find this so crazy: they are willing to risk letting me go to UCSD for a title," she wrote.

She was ready to leave. She was tired of fighting, and she wasn't really any good at it. What good was getting angry if she inevitably backed down too early when pushed back? She hadn't yet figured out how to refuse to leave the table.

"I would love to go to UCSD, but I will surely miss Freya," she wrote. "Will have to see UCSD 8/19-8/22."

The chairman of the department of surgery, an elegantly dressed man who reminded her of Omar Sharif, ushered her into his office. Courtly and solicitous, he ticked off the reasons he wanted her to come to San Diego. "We realize women are very important in breast surgery," he said. "If you have a woman you have an edge."

His approach was the exact opposite of her superiors at Columbia. He made Reemstma look like a deadweight in her eyes. Reemstma had been a highly regarded surgeon—he pioneered using nonhuman organs in transplant operations and developed a mechanical heart program—but he operated infrequently now. The San

Diego chairman had a reputation as an excellent surgeon, and he operated all the time. He would have real knowledge of the daily logistical obstacles faced by his surgeons. The salary of $250,000 was about half her current income but the cut did not concern her. What was important was the sense that San Diego really wanted her. She could rebuild her practice, pumping up her billings over time if she wanted. Alison told him that although she was interested she would not even consider moving if her husband could not also find a job. He said he thought the hospital could work something out.

Over the next three days Alison had back-to-back meetings scheduled, and when she returned to Columbia she described the environment there as "paradise" to Schnabel. The doctors were young, smart, and friendly, unlike their stuffy colleagues at Columbia. Being a woman just didn't figure into the conversation, other than as a plus, she said. It was a topnotch research facility, better than Columbia. They all seemed enthusiastic about their work, she said, yet also seemed to have the time to go windsurfing in the morning and to lunch by the pool. She said one doctor told her "life is a blast."

Deeply unnerved by the prospect of Alison's moving, Schnabel pointed out that she was sure it wasn't the only offer Alison was going to get. Other jobs, better jobs, would come along. Alison was among a small pool of breast surgeons prominent in academic medicine, and she hadn't even reached her peak yet. But even as she made these arguments, Schnabel understood the attraction. Here Alison was working like a dog, putting in 60 and more hours a week, frustrated with everything from the poorly managed operating-room schedule to the pathology department, while in San Diego the doctors were surfer surgeons and they wanted her. Even before San Diego was put on the table, Alison and Schnabel had talked a lot about working too hard and about their desire to have a life outside the hospital. San Diego represented that. Life could be a blast.

Over the next several weeks, when something went wrong, Alison and Schnabel locked eyes. "Life is a blast," one of them would repeat to the other, laughing.

For some time, her friend Jennifer Patterson had been urging Alison to enlist some of her well-connected patients to plead her case. But she knew Alison felt uncomfortable asking for help—or using people, as Alison would see it. It wasn't in her nature. But Alison was tolerant of too many things, Patterson thought, and politically naïve. That had hurt her. She did not know her own worth, and in the process she had allowed Columbia not to recognize it either. Because Alison had not forced Columbia's hand, she had created an environment in which Columbia could continue to try to recruit a big-name surgeon while she worked herself to the bone. Practically speaking, why should Columbia want to change the status quo? Alison was Cinderella, ever faithful, ever hardworking. She was too modest. Now that it looked like Alison might go to San Diego, Patterson decided it was time to intercede.

At a cocktail party, Patterson approached one of Alison's high-profile patients, a woman whom she knew socially. The woman was prominent in media and political circles, and her word would carry great weight. Patterson told her that Alison was considering going to San Diego because she was unhappy at Columbia. Was there anything she could do?

At her next appointment, the woman broached the subject with Alison. "This is terrible," she said. "Just ask for what you want." She said she was going to call some friends on the hospital's board of trustees to complain.

Alison thought the woman had no idea had difficult it was to fight in these situations, but she saw it couldn't hurt to talk about it.

Alison next mentioned her possible departure during dinner with a woman friend and two other women, friends and breast-cancer patients of Alison's. The host, who'd also had breast cancer, was the wife of a lawyer who worked for the Milsteins, but Alison had never mentioned her problems, worried that it might not be fair to involve her. As Alison explained her reasoning, the host became more and more exercised. She hadn't been one of Alison's patients, but she knew scores of women who were, and every one of them was crazy about her. She couldn't understand why Columbia wasn't making a big deal out of having a woman as chief of the breast division. It was an obvious plus, she said. She was going to talk to her husband and urge him to speak to Alison and to Milstein.

Shortly after the dinner, Alison spoke with the woman's husband. He said he had some general knowledge about the doctors' complaints and about her earlier salary problems. "Jesus, this is terrible. You're really getting screwed," he said. He would try to help her, he said, but he thought she would be far more effective if she took her case to one of the Milstein daughters, who was actively involved with the hospital. The senior Milstein, he said, was probably as much a part of the old boy network as anybody, but he was fair-minded. If somebody could explain your case and show why the decision to search for a chief should be reversed you probably would be successful, he said. "Go to her," he said.

A few days after she returned from San Diego, Alison met with a woman oncologist who was planning to come to Columbia to become the Director of Oncology. The oncologist asked Alison about the number of patients Alison might be able to refer to her. Alison told her she was seriously thinking about accepting the job offer in San Diego. "This is really bad," the oncologist said. She urged Alison to discuss it with the dean of the medical school, Herbert Pardes, who as Reemstma's superior was responsible for hiring decisions. Michelle Friedman, Alison's psychiatrist friend, also had been prodding Alison to see Pardes for some time. Because he was a psychiatrist and he had a long-time relationship with a dedicated and prominent female scientist, she thought he would be sympathetic to Alison. He was a decent human being, Friedman said. "Lay the whole thing out," she had told Alison. He will get it.

What did she have to lose? Being a good soldier and obeying the chain of command hadn't done her much good so far. If nothing else, she knew that Pardes would be troubled because she was bringing in more money than anyone else in general surgery. The dean's job was to look at the bottom line. She called that day and made an appointment.

Sitting in his large office at the conference table, Alison reeled off her litany of reasons for considering the San Diego job. She told him everything. She complained about the search for a replacement, including the gynecologist's comments about women surgeons.

Pardes, 58, had made some inquiries after Alison's call and had heard about the gynecologist's complaints. He had no tolerance for that kind of attitude, and if he had heard about it earlier, he would have gotten involved right away. He told Alison he was well aware that a woman surgeon was bound to encounter problems, because surgeons were known to be chauvinistic. It had to be hard, he told her. He asked how many women were in the surgery department. Alison said two—herself and Schnabel. "It's rough here," she told him. "These guys are on my back."

The dean asked her to put her problems in writing and to speak with him before she made any decisions. The hospital did not want to lose her. He thought she was an outstanding academic surgeon. Finally she had found a responsive ear.

Pardes picked up the phone to find Reemstma. He normally tried to let people run their department, but this time he thought it was important to intervene. The hospital could not afford to lose Alison. Besides, if Reemstma was being pressured by others not to appoint her then Pardes could act as the buffer. Reemstma could say the dean made him do it. One way or another, this had gone too far.

• • •

Reemstma, who was in Joseph, Oregon on vacation and business, stopped at a gas station to use the pay phone. He had just spoken to the dean, who in no uncertain terms had told him to make Alison's position permanent and to make sure she stayed at Columbia. Pardes had made it clear he wanted action taken now, today. Reemstma thought Alison was reacting too strongly to the delay in her appointment, and putting a disproportionate emphasis on things that usually were not taken that seriously. Most people in the surgery department don't decide to go someplace else because an appointment was taking longer than they expected. Reemstma dialed Alison's number. He said he wanted her to know how much he appreciated her work and did not want her to leave. She ran the best service in the hospital and he was calling off the search for a replacement. She was officially the permanent chief of the breast service, he said. They set up a meeting for August 31, 1992, to make it official with the dean, Alison, and Reemstma.

Alison's reaction was bittersweet. She had finally won, but the two-year battle had been demoralizing and draining. She had always liked the actual work at Columbia—the contact with patients, the programs—but if she stayed she would still have to work with the same people who had demeaned her.

That night she typed out a memo. "I want three things," she wrote. At the top of her list was an explanation of the search for Chief of Breast Surgery. She wanted to know why Reemstma and the committee chairman had told her that the committee felt the search should continue, contrary to what her friends on the committee had said. She wanted to know why the doctor affiliated with the federal research center was being considered for the chief of Oncology/Breast when "he has very little interest in breast, is younger than I, and has no publications in breast surgery? Roman Nowygrod, Chief of General Surgery, told me on multiple occasions that I would then be demoted to Assistant Director, or Assistant Chief, of Breast Surgery." Next on her list was "in writing the title of uncontested Chief of Breast Surgery." And finally she wanted a change in how her salary was configured. In addition to paying her own expenses, she currently gave the hospital's surgery department 20 percent of her fees. She wanted to reduce her portion to 15 percent and have half of that go directly back to the breast service.

In another memo, she wrote that she also wanted assurances that the hospital would hire a scientist to study breast cancer, and that she would participate in the recruitment. "This is probably the most important component of an academic center," she stated. She wanted to be able to hire another breast surgeon in the next two years, and she wanted money to pay a tumor registrar, to support her own lab and possibly to pay for a physician's assistant. In return for their assurances in writing that Alison was the permanent chief, Nowygrod asked Alison to put in writing that she would stay at Columbia. He did not want to go out on a limb and drop the search only to have Alison later say she wasn't going to stay. Alison ignored the request. She finally had the upper hand.

In the interim, Reemstma met with the gynecologist over lunch to break the news. "You can be assured that there will always be male surgeons in my department who are able to handle problems with breast disease," Reemstma later recalled saying, "There will also be female surgeons who handle this, and the chief of this service is going to be a female."

The chairman of the surgery department at San Diego was still calling all the time, appealing to her to take the job. Other doctors called too, including some Alison didn't even know. Schnabel joked it was like rush week at a sorority. The appeal of San Diego was obvious to Schnabel. Everyone at San Diego was focused on winning Alison, pursuing her intently, while the doctors at Columbia took her for granted.

After Alison and Bill flew to San Diego in December to meet with hospital officials and to look at houses, a colleague told Alison that Reemstma again had approached David Kinne, the Memorial–Sloan Kettering surgeon, to ask him to reconsider coming to Columbia. Reemstma later called to assure Alison not to worry, she would still be chief. He had told Kinne the same thing. Though she had no problem with Kinne's arriving, she found it demeaning that Reemstma would recruit someone without first consulting her. She thought she had the upper hand, but now it seemed virtually nothing had changed. Was she only going to be chief in name, not authority? She'd won the battle, but she couldn't help doubting that her superiors at Columbia would ever believe that having a woman as the head of a women's service was a good idea, even though Reemstma insisted he believed this.

Alison liked to make quick decisions and then move on, but she found herself increasingly indecisive about going to San Diego. Did she really want to go to San Diego or was she running away, taking the easy way out?

Michelle Friedman, her friend who was also a psychiatrist, advised her that she was having difficulty because she was making a much larger decision than just a choice about a career or an academic path. This was a life choice that would determine her future, or at least the next phase of it, and Alison needed to examine methodically its impact on each of the important areas of her life. Look at how the move is going to affect your relationship with Bill, your relationships with your family and your friends. Look at what you like and don't like about both jobs. Michelle worried that Alison was caught up in the contrast between the two places— knocking herself out and commuting to a slumlike place where people treated her terribly, when in beautiful sunny California people thought she was great. Make sure you're not considering the job just to get back at Columbia and in the process cutting off your nose to spite your face, Michelle warned her.

Alison first considered its impact on Bill and their marriage. On the one hand, she hoped the move might be better for Bill, because San Diego had made him a nice offer, coming up with a higher-paying job for him in a laboratory that was superior to his at Yale. But on the other, she knew, as he did, that she was the one the hospital wanted, and he was understandably fearful of what the change would mean for him. If his job did not work out, the marriage probably would suffer. They did not have the romance of the century, but she wanted her marriage to stay together. He was extremely tolerant of her work habits, even boastful that she earned so much more than he did. "This is my wife, she paid for my car; this is my wife, she paid for our house," he often joked when he introduced Alison. His flexibility gave her more options. She knew other men might not find it easy being married to her.

The idea of leaving her friends and family also terrified her. What would she do on weekends or on weekday nights without Jennifer Patterson or Michelle Friedman? Patterson had adopted a baby and asked Alison to be the godmother. She saw or spoke to her father, who lived in Greenwich Village, every week, and she was extremely close to her sister ZuZu, an art curator at the Guggenheim, who had spent the past year in Holland but was scheduled to return soon. She had spent a week alone in Block Island once with no one to talk to except the dog, and couldn't stand the loneliness. What would happen to Schnabel? What about the other people she'd hired, like the young woman, a former secretary in the office, whom she had helped become a physician's assistant. Alison considered her a good friend. Was it fair to bring them in and then leave?

Alison reported to Friedman that the pros and cons lists balanced each other out. Friedman gave her the name of a psychiatrist who specialized in helping people make career changes. Alison made an appointment in February 1993, but she found the session useless. The psychiatrist seemed to flip and flop as much as she did, swaying to whatever argument she made, and seemed not to appreciate why she might like her current arrangement of spending two nights a week apart from her husband. He suggested she enter into therapy to discover why she valued so much being away from him.

She left his office, annoyed that she was no closer to making a decision than before she saw him. She decided not to go back, almost as exasperated with him as she was with herself.

As the months wore on, other factors prolonged her indecision. David Kinne finally decided to come to Columbia and Reemstma kept his promise, creating a new position for Kinne rather than making him the chief of breast service. Kinne had not yet officially arrived, but he had come to one of Alison's tumor board meetings and she had found his presence comforting. A question arose about treatment and everyone looked at Alison, as they always did. She gave her opinion and then, turning to Kinne, said, "What do you think?" She now finally had someone else to rely on for advice in tough cases. Before making any decisions about San Diego, she wanted to see how Kinne would work out.

She'd also heard that the chairman of the surgery department at San Diego might be leaving, creating a period of turmoil and uncertainty there. What if she decided to go and her chief supporter was gone? She might be out of a job. She'd have to wait and watch.

The calls from San Diego continued at a feverish pitch into May, and Alison still had not yet made a decision. She'd heard recently that the position of the San Diego chairman was more uncertain than ever, but she wasn't ready to let go of her fantasies about California, even if she knew it wasn't fair to stall forever. A week before the Memorial Day weekend, she and Bill hashed out the advantages and disadvantages one more time. She was getting nowhere. He finally said, "I am going to make the decision for you. We're not going."

He listed the reasons why they should stay: "You're really a New Yorker. You will miss your friends too much. You will be very sad out there. The hospital is a rinky-dink place compared to Columbia and you're still going to be chief."

Bill was right. If the chairman ended up leaving, she might also be out of a job. To uproot for this kind of uncertainty was insane. Alison felt the anxiety lift. She called the dean at San Diego's medical school. He asked her to reconsider. He told her they would do anything to get her to come out there short of moving the hospital to New York. Five minutes later, the chairman of the San Diego surgery department paged her. He left his home number, his beeper number, and his office number. But she did not want to talk to him then. Not yet fully comfortable with her decision, she wanted to mull it over.

She and Bill traveled to Block Island for the long weekend, and on Saturday Alison picked up the phone to call the chairman. She knew he had a graduation to oversee and would not be able to speak long. He said he would call her on Monday.

Later, sitting outside, feeling the ocean breeze and staring at the water, Alison began to reconsider. Life in New York did not seem quite so appealing. She was forty-one and medicine had taught her that anything could go wrong suddenly. "Maybe we should go out there," Bill said, sensing her change of heart.

On Monday, the chairman called again. "I really want you to come," he said. "Come back one last time," he asked. "If you still don't like it we'll leave you alone."

• • •

By her second day in San Diego, Alison could see the hospital was pulling out all the stops to convince her to take the job. Each meeting seemed designed to appeal to a different interest, and eliminate any doubts. The dean of the medical school assured her the chairman's future would not affect her, as the university had guaranteed her job and her salary, and he showed her a letter to that effect. During another meeting, a three-hour lunch with doctors and researchers affiliated with the hospital's cancer center, each gave formal presentations about their research and budgets, with a particular focus on the role Alison could play. Alison no longer expected to conduct high-level research herself, but she wanted to contribute to people who did. The center had just received a large federal grant and been selected to participate in the federal Women's Health Initiative, a cutting-edge research project. The best and most up-to-date treatment depended on research, an area where Alison thought Columbia was failing, at least in breast-cancer research. She resented that she felt she had to send some patients to other hospitals like Duke University's to get the best medical care. San Diego's state-of-the-art computer systems also made Columbia's record keeping look primitive. To make up for Columbia's inadequacies Alison had been personally paying the salary of a registrar to tabulate the demographic and pathologic data on breast-cancer patients. How could a surgeon learn anything if she did not know the numbers? Even Bill, who was hardly ever overwhelmed, told Alison he was impressed.

At a separate meeting with the staff at the women's health center, a newly renovated building near the hospital, the doctors and administrators begged her to come. They were desperate to have an expert, they said, because the male surgeons currently operating on breast-cancer patients were not primarily breast surgeons.

Even though she did not think she needed to earn as much as she did at Columbia, she had learned the lesson that value increased with income and had told the San Diego administrators the original offer was too low. Before they left San Diego, hospital administrators sweetened their offer. They guaranteed Bill a job at $100,000 a year for two years—his current salary had been slashed almost in half because of funding problems—and raised Alison's salary offer to $375,000.

Alison, however, was not completely starry-eyed. Health maintenance organizations were making huge inroads in San Diego because they provided medical services more cheaply than traditional fee-for-service medicine. Some of the statements used by administrators were ones she'd heard often enough in New York to call it the "Columbia Syndrome"—a wrong-headed belief that patients would continue to come to the hospital even if the costs were higher because their doctors had good reputations. She knew they would eventually drift away, and without the income from patient billings she would be unable to build her division or hire assistants. The hospital's financial administrator assured her the hospital was in the process of adjusting its procedure.

Back at Columbia everything looked terrible in comparison. The operating room rarely ran on schedule. Support staff had been cut by layoffs. "Thank God I'm getting out of here," she said to herself one day when she had to wait an hour just for instruments to be sterilized, forcing an equally long delay of an operation. "I hate this place."

At the end of September, Bill flew to San Diego at Alison's urging to meet separately with hospital officials and give a talk on his area of expertise—recurrent brain tumors in young children. Though she was leaning toward going, she would not move unless Bill was satisfied with his job. Because he tended to be reticent, she worried she had done too much of the talking for him in their last visit and neither side had gotten a good feel for the other. He needed to establish his own relationships if the move was going to work out. She expected she would be fine, but what if they decided they hated Bill after two years and sent him packing?

Midway through his stay, Bill called to report that his presentation and interviews were going well, but he said he remained unsure about the move. He would not have his own laboratory or a slot on the rotation to look at his own slides. He also would have to perform a large number of autopsies, a prospect that did not please him.

Around the same time, Alison met for dinner with a surgeon visiting New Jersey from San Diego. He said he'd also been recruited to San Diego with big promises, but they had failed to materialize. His list of complaints was long. The dominance of health maintenance organizations, and the hospital's lack of response to them, was killing him. He'd performed only a fraction of the number of surgeries he'd been led to expect, and was still sharing a secretary and working out of a temporary office in a trailer. He painted a portrait of disorganization and instability.

Shortly after Bill returned, he laid out his concerns. Not only was he worried about his own job, she was giving up a great position at Columbia for half the salary.

The whole University of California system was being ravaged by funding cuts, and it threatened only to get worse. He thought they should stay.

Alison was not going to move without Bill's full endorsement, especially if factors beyond her control might prevent her from building a practice. Her work at Columbia—when she separated it from her personal feelings about her superiors—was going exceedingly well, better than ever. She and Schnabel continued to expand the breast service, and Kinne's arrival had created an environment of intellectual rigor. She decided not to take the job in San Diego.

Before informing anyone of her decision, however, Alison decided to take stock of her life. She did not want to reject the offer and return to her life as usual, as if the turmoil of the past 18 months hadn't occurred. Something had propelled her to want to move. Did she need to make changes in her life?

First, other than the obvious appeal of being wanted and the doctors' receptivity to women there, she had found the work at San Diego immensely appealing because research was alive and exciting. Second, she had gravitated to change and adventure throughout her life, and part of San Diego's allure was simply being exposed to new people and different ideas, different cultures. After 15 years, the sameness of Columbia, of the routine, had begun to bore her. Finally, she recognized that she had hoped the move would enrich her relationship with Bill, bring them closer together. Even though she'd been

annoyed when the psychiatrist suggested she enter therapy to figure out why she was wary of giving up her two
nights a week alone, she realized her reluctance perhaps
signaled a growing distance, and it was important for
them to try to spend more time together.

Having identified what appealed to her about the
move, she decided to take some steps to improve her life
at Columbia. To fulfill her desire to do more research,
she decided to apply for some of the $210 million the
U.S. Department of Defense had received from Congress
to study breast cancer. She also decided that she wanted
to take a six-month sabbatical to find out what other hospitals were doing in breast cancer and bring herself completely up to date. She would physically be away from
Columbia for a month of travel in the United States and
abroad to breast-cancer centers. The rest of the time she
would continue to see old patients, but not accept any
new ones. The sabbatical would fulfill her need for a
change and an adventure, give her time to think, allow
her to make a contribution to the science of breast cancer, and stimulate her intellectually.

Next, she talked to Bill about finding a house closer to
Yale or his finding a job closer to their house in New Jersey, either of which would increase the amount of time
they spent together. They also would proceed with plans
to build a second home on Block Island in Rhode Island,
at least temporarily gaining some of the scenic beauty
and tranquillity of life by the sea.

Alison's final step was to tell Reemstma and
Nowygrod that she was staying, but that she wanted to
take a sabbatical. Seemingly delighted, Reemstma said
she had been working too hard and he did not want her
to burn out. The sabbatical sounded like a great idea. Al-

ison was under no illusion that her superiors were suddenly enlightened, but for now she could accept them as long as they did not stand in her way. She finally had reached the point at Columbia where she could do what she wanted, and ignore the rest.

A Concluding Word

Shortly before Alison decided not to go to San Diego, she wrote me a letter. We had just spent a couple of days together, and she wanted to tell me, she said, that our discussion had prodded her to evaluate what in her life satisfied her and what did not. "I have spent some time thinking about the various things we spoke about, especially family dynamics, life goals, and best and worst times," she wrote. That she had continued to think about our talks did not surprise me. During our conversation, her recollections had tumbled out, seeming to catch even her by surprise, and when I had dropped her at the airport the last time she had seemed pensive, as if still caught in the trance of memory.

More than two years had passed since I met Alison on a summer night in New York, a few months after I started research on this book. Since then I had come to associate her cream-colored stationery, periodically found in my mailbox, with the promise of sharing with me her own inner ruminations. I liked the fact that she did not shrink from taking a hard look at herself. Tucking her letter back into its envelope, I felt a twinge of sadness. My interviews were nearing an end, and I knew I would miss my extended conversations with Alison, Rachael, and Meredith. I did not pretend to be either psychiatrist or priest. Still, I felt I knew them more intimately than I knew most people because I had examined their lives closely and asked questions of them that I would be hesitant to explore even with my closest friends. Never have I had a talk with any friend like the one I had about sex and masturbation with Rachael. Though my goals were strictly journalistic, I felt I had entered their lives as substantially more than an observer.

As I wrote this book I was often asked by other women why I thought Meredith, Alison, and Rachael consented to expose themselves so fully and with such apparent candor. Talking about inner conflicts seemed to promise little obvious gain, and much peril, especially for women who lived such public lives and had husbands and family to consider, not to mention employers. Why would a woman talk about her struggles if doing so threatened to rattle the already fragile foundations of her life? These questioners doubted they would ever share their frustrations, regardless of how deep their distress.

I knew from my work as a reporter that a subject sometimes agrees to talk because it is flattering to have a journalist interested in your life; it bestows a sense of importance. Who else hangs on your every word, as if everything you say is significant? Others want to settle a score. But I also knew that, for most people, that early sensation of trust or excitement dissipates once a reporter inches closer to the personal questions. Withdrawal and distance settle in. I worried this would happen to me here. I was not conducting an investigation into these women's lives, but I'd made it clear I was going to write about their innermost struggles. A tape recorder often sat on the table, spinning away silently but visible as a reminder. That they continued to talk rather than call a halt to this process underscored what I had begun to suspect was impelling them to talk, a hunch Alison confirmed in a January 1993 letter. "Although I probably would have questioned the happenings in the Surgery Department, I would have felt less secure than I did (and do now)," she wrote, adding that our talks had left her feeling "braver." Their interests and mine, though separate, had begun to coincide. I was interested in writing a narrative, and they were interested in trying to resolve some of their inner conflicts. But the process of talking honestly about their lives served both ends: it gave me the taboo-breaking material I was seeking; and it helped them to change their lives. They discovered, as I did, a central lesson: If a woman speaks candidly about her life, even when it means revealing deep distress, the process itself can lead to awareness and, possibly, a means to control conflicts that otherwise only amplify with time and silence.

"It can be very damaging to say what you think because a lot of people don't want to know that you're having a hard time, especially on a professional level, so I always want to put the best face forward," Meredith explained one morning, midway through a tearful discussion. "But how do you if it's really impossible and you're struggling? I don't understand ultimately what you gain because you are perpetuating a lie. And therefore, if it's okay, (people will say) 'You can take more of the same, dear,' and you're stuck in it, more and more."

I do not mean to suggest here that Alison, Rachael, and Meredith talked easily and readily about all areas of their lives, gushing forth like a dam suddenly unplugged. Anyone who has ever probed the quality and direction of her own life, much less someone else's, knows that all self-examination inevitably proceeds slowly and fitfully, often with two steps forward and then one backward. This kind of introspection can be particularly difficult for women, because they frequently have been conditioned to think first of others' emotions before clarifying their own, whether or not they are accomplished women like these three. These three women found it particularly hard to acknowledge distress and frustration in their family lives because they care a great deal about their husbands and children.

Rachael, for example, insisted to me for nearly a year that she felt loved and embraced as the first lady of West Virginia before breaking down and admitting that she actually had cried half the time during that period, almost bereft, feeling deeply alone and friendless in Charleston, with a dwindling number of guest-conducting appearances. Even after she acknowledged her life was less than the fairy tale she presented to the public, Rachael worried that her comments might reflect negatively on Gaston and hurt his position in the state.

Meredith spoke hesitantly about her strained relationship with her mother and talked reluctantly about Richard's illness, fearful she might cause her mother pain or jeopardize Richard's employment prospects. But each time one of the women finally broached a sensitive area, the benefit of speaking honestly again became apparent. I could see the tension slowly lift, as if she had withheld this piece of important information also from herself. Having finally given voice to this one piece of truth seemed to enable her to see her life more clearly, and provide an impetus to address it.

Virginia Woolf understood the effect when she wrote about a painful incident in her life. "By putting it into words," she wrote, "I make it whole; this wholeness means it has lost its power to hurt me."

Even when they were ready to speak candidly, getting to the truth was still often difficult and protracted because emotions and feelings were often buried and suppressed. Being intelligent was no guarantee that a woman had spent enough time examining her own underlying feelings. What sometimes seemed like a given turned out to be a partial screen, behind which another reason rested. Meredith, for example, said she signed on as the early-morning news anchor because her children needed her. At first I accepted that as true, then I began to detect in interviews with other women that many who had cited their responsibility to be a "good mother" as the reason for dropping out or curtailing their careers also had other more-complicated explanations. Many, I discovered, felt an unexpected ambivalence toward their careers, even if they achieved at high levels, and saw their children as a more real and vital source of identity. Being at the center of the family made them feel needed. When their jobs forced them to yield significant responsibilities to their husbands or others they felt shunted aside, on the periphery of the family.

About a year after we had met, I asked Meredith if she agreed. She paused and then nodded. She did not like to admit it, she said, but she disliked having to share her parenting responsibilities with Richard or a nanny because she wanted to be the emotional center of the family, the one everyone depended on. How had the household managed when she was absent on a reporting trip? I asked. She looked at me with as much pain as I had seen in all the time we spoke. "It functioned very well," she said, softly crying.

I had a similar experience with Rachael, who nine months and several interviews after we first sat down announced hesitantly that she had something she wanted to tell me. "We are thinking about adopting a baby," she said. We had talked about children in every one of our interviews, and in each Rachael insisted she did not want children. Gaston, she had told me, had even undergone a vasectomy at her request shortly after their marriage. Now, after a moment of silence, I asked what had changed. "Over the course of speaking with you, being interviewed by you, and having certain questions arise, and listening to myself in response, I've realized that in a number of the areas about which we've spoken I'm giving you the same answer that I've given myself," she said. "And I've always promised myself that I would be a person who reevaluated my thinking on a regular basis and I would always be in the process of thinking." She said she could let her answers lie as far as my research was concerned, but she could not let them remain unchallenged by herself. Listening to herself then led to her next stage: her revelation that one of her largest obstacles to having a baby was fear of her mother's reaction.

Learning to distinguish which obstacles came from the outside—other people or situations—and which from within was one of the important by-products these women gained. It is apparent from their stories that external obstacles played significant roles in their dissatisfaction, from the work-is-the-only-thing-that-matters culture at *60 Minutes* to sexism in the worlds of classical music, politics, and surgery. But focusing alone on those was not going to get the women anywhere. However intractable and unjust the realities, the interior reasons were equally, if not more, important, because in the end the women themselves had responsibility for their individual satisfaction. No one else was going to provide it for them.

But learning to tell the difference by telling the truth was not enough. As the poet and essayist Adrienne Rich wrote, "The awakening of consciousness is not like the crossing of a frontier—one step and you are in another country." The next step was finding ways to avoid repeating the patterns that had caused the pain in the first place, and that could only be accomplished by making changes.

In the midst of writing this book I read a description written by the author Doris Kearns Goodwin of a seminar given by the psychologist Erik Erikson on the critical importance of finding balance in life. After a lifetime of studying human development, Erikson said he had found that those who pursued work, love, and play in equal measure were those most likely to attain inner balance and to live the richest and fullest lives, while those who concentrated on one area to the exclusion of the others were most likely to feel unhappy as the years passed. I remember agreeing as I read the description. The women I had interviewed frequently failed to find balance in their lives, and I believed a lot of their unhappiness stemmed from this.

But as I thought about Erikson's observation in relationship to these women I also began to think it was not specific or inclusive enough of all the areas in a woman's life. I had seen from my own experience that a woman was happiest when she devoted time and attention to each of the measures I mentioned in my introduction—work, love, children and family, friends, time for self, sense of place, and sense of self—and was sad and disappointed when she ignored one or several, or failed to understand the importance of one in making an important decision about her life.

Meredith discovered the consequences of ignoring her own need for meaningful work when she accepted the morning anchor job in order to spend more time with her children; her anxiety and frustration spilled over into every area of her life. Not only did she lose confidence in herself as a professional, she had little time for her marriage, she rarely saw her friends, and she had no time for herself. Alison's closest friends believed her struggle at Columbia was heightened because work dominated her life, leaving little room for anything else. Rachael relied too much on Gaston to change her life, and she had been naïve to believe that she would not spend a great deal of time in West Virginia as the wife of the governor, in spite of what Gaston's friends might have assured her. Forsaking a more cosmpolitan setting like New York had proven difficult for her, but in refusing to accept West Virginia for what it was, she had exacerbated her alienation and the tension and loneliness of living in a strange land. When I thought about Rachael in West Virginia I often thought about a line in E. M. Forster's *Where Angels Fear to Tread:* "I and my life must be where I live."

I do not like to invoke the imagined Everywoman, because the more I learn about women the more I believe in idiosyncrasy and individuality. But I believe some of the failure to find balance does have to do with the general nature of being a woman. Nearly three decades after the modern women's movement began, the women I interviewed still tended to ask themselves, in one form or another: Am I giving enough? They often felt uncomfortable integrating their own needs with those of others, particularly when it came to setting limits in working and loving. Even when they felt they could not give any more, boundaries were almost impossible to set because they felt it was their job to serve others. Meredith believed she should make herself continually available to her children when she also knew she should be working. Alison accepted patients when she was worn-out and agonized over what would happen to her staff if she left for San Diego. And Rachael spent hours on relatively unimportant duties as first lady because she felt no one else could take her place and she owed it to Gaston.

Each time one of the women confronted a conflict in one of the major areas of her life, she often felt she had to choose between one side and the other and necessarily came up short, unable to figure out a way to order her priorities so that nothing need be sacrificed. "It splits my life," Rachael said of trying to be first lady and a conductor. She felt she had to get out of the state to live her real life. Meredith said another time, "I've never felt comfortable sharing myself." Alison considered taking a leave of absence from her job when she felt she had no time for herself, her friends, or her family. It was as if these women at times had "no dimmer switch," as Meredith's husband, Richard Cohen, described Meredith's inability to cope with crisis without feeling she had to completely interrupt one part of her life to deal with another. Richard, in contrast, could shut the door of their home office and work, and Gaston could pick up the pieces of his disappointment and campaign with vigor. It wasn't that Richard or Gaston cared less, but that they could tolerate conflict better.

Attaining balance does not mean being able to "have it all," as the cliché goes. "Nothing works best" is a mantra that each woman needed to repeat until she not only understood it but also embraced its corollary—making compromises—as a healthy approach to living. Even though these women intellectually understood the concept, too often they seemed to be torturing themselves by requiring perfection, and instead found themselves mired in guilt, convinced they could do nothing right. Whether they had children or not was almost insignificant when it came to feeling they had failed to live up to their own expectations. Even when Meredith, Rachael, or Alison knew a choice had to be made, it was a source of perpetual conflict and would propel an inward debate as to whether that choice represented a wise sacrifice or a fundamental failing.

Deciding not to have children, or to turn down a job promotion, can be a positive choice that will bring happiness, but the decision has to be made out of self-confidence, not as a result of external pressures. When you feel forced to let something go in order to relieve pressure, other problems usually ensue, as Meredith discovered when she left *60 Minutes* for the morning anchor job. With fewer responsibilities came less authority and less influence. Leaving *60 Minutes* was not the wrong decision; taking the morning show was. Sometimes the greater the level of conflict a woman can tolerate the more freedom she retains, and this is where the concept of balance can be useful as a tool and not just an abstraction. Alison agonized over turning down the job offer from San Diego and staying at Columbia, but it probably was the right decision. She weighed the move's impact on all the areas of her life. Finding the negatives to outweigh the advantages, she took what she learned from that self-examination and came up with a plan to make her life better at Columbia, and with her husband. I think she made a similarly wise choice not to have children. For a woman to say, "I am searching for a good-enough life" is not failure, but maturity and self-knowledge. Sometimes walking around the mountain, rather than scaling it, is the wisest route to take.

My aim in writing this book was not to cover the entire lives of my subjects. I specifically confined each chapter to a limited time because I wanted to look at how a woman dealt with a concentrated conflict. I did, however, speak over a much longer period with each of the women and kept up with them afterward. At this writing, Meredith, Rachael, and Alison seem on the road to more satisfying lives—better able to make the necessary choices to deal with old conflicts and newly emerging ones, rather than waiting for things to happen to them. They had become more aggressive in taking responsibility for their own happiness.

Meredith had found a job that enabled her to spend time with her children and derive more fulfillment from her work than her morning anchor position did. Her bosses at ABC and *Turning Point* had kept their commitment to allow her to do almost all her work from home and to travel only five days a month, and she was able to produce first-rate pieces about subjects that mattered to her. Among her best were a year-long look at the experiences of a mentally retarded child enrolled in a regular classroom, and a story about the treatment of children with cancer. Though the traveling was still tough, the trade-off in professional satisfaction was worth the cost and helped her relax her control over the household, and feel more comfortable accepting Richard as an equal partner as a parent.

Richard, in the interim, had begun a new job as the producer of a cable talk show hosted by Jane Wallace, and often left the house early in the morning and did not return until 9:30 at night. Feeling better about her own life, Meredith reacted to their new situation more maturely and less anxiously than she would have approached it in the past. Although they had less time together as a couple, she welcomed the alleviation of the financial pressure and knew their relationship was still better than during her days on the morning show when the constant fatigue eliminated any enjoyment they might have shared. Because she had flexibility in her own schedule the juggling and stress that otherwise might have occurred also was blunted.

It was, however, unclear how much longer Meredith's arrangement would last. In November 1994, ABC announced it was canceling *Turning Point* as a regular weekly series and rescheduling it as a series of periodic specials, despite the show's good ratings and critical acclaim. At the time, she had two years to go on her contract and reassurances from ABC executives that they wanted her to continue working on *Turning Point*. But in reality she knew the show's future was in jeopardy, as was her own. ABC executives already had started talking to her about appearing on some of their other magazine shows, and she worried that the show's emphasis would change by becoming a series of specials. Pieces like her one about the mentally retarded child probably would become less salable, while high-profile subjects like O.J. Simpson would become more the norm. She decided if it came to that she would find something else to do, and it would not include working on another magazine show that broadcast 12-minute pieces, even if it meant giving up such a large salary. She had struggled to reach that decision, but having made it she felt at peace. She no longer wanted that kind of life or that kind of exposure. The angst she felt in leaving *60 Minutes* about not being at the top was much less, if not gone.

Rachael began confronting her mother more directly, yet less contentiously, and pulling back from her state duties to concentrate on her music. Her work paid off in some guest-conducting positions, including her European debut in 1994. But she was still struggling to move on to a bigger job in this country, and she was pained when her critics in West Virginia waged an intense yet ultimately unsuccessful campaign to block her nomination by President Clinton to a national arts council. Because of the uncertainty of her career direction, she had not yet made a decision about adopting a child.

Alison, who seemed to have learned the most from her self-examination, was firmly in place as the chief of breast surgery and starting to ignore what she could not change. She hired two new breast surgeons, including a close woman friend. In the fall of 1994, a new surgeon took over the department of surgery, and his presence has made a world of difference to her. He was only a year older than she and they had been colleagues for years. He regularly referred to the past as a "chauvinist time period" and complimented her in private and in public, holding up her division as a model for others in the hospital to follow. Her husband, Bill, has switched jobs to a hospital nearer their home, bringing them closer together and eliminating the need to buy a new house. They also had begun to discuss spending 1997 working as doctors in a third world country, a lifetime goal of hers.

In the interim, her national reputation continued to grow. She was asked in March 1995 if she would consider taking over the breast service at a large hospital in Boston affiliated with Harvard University. When told the hospital was interested solely in finding a woman chief, she was now able to laugh. She did not think, however, that she would pursue the job. She was content for now.

The changes naturally brought new disruptions and uncertainty. As Meredith said, "Once you make a choice it is not always easier, even if you realize or intellectualize it. You still have to live with all kinds of emotions. . . . That could be a lifetime dilemma."

There is much work still ahead for the women. One of the few givens of human nature is that no one, woman or man, is ever going to resolve all inner conflict. But these women had learned, as I hope others have from their stories, that the anxiety caused by change can be cured only by more change, and that change for a woman often means taking responsibility to find balance in her life. It means insisting on meaningful work as well as meaningful time with husbands, friends, children, and parents. It means carving out time alone and creating an environment in which to flourish. It means taking seriously the need to clarify beliefs, priorities, and life goals. It also means telling the truth about secret sadnesses and hidden aspirations.

Writing has always helped me clarify my own thoughts and emotions, and writing this book has been no different. As I write now, for example, I understand that the questions I asked these three women were questions I was also asking myself. They were my window into the female condition, but I see now that they were also a window into myself.

I was 34 when I began my research, only a few years younger than my subjects, and looking for answers in my own life. I was married to a man I loved deeply and getting paid to do something I'd wanted to do since I was a child—write. I did not have children, and though I'd insisted for years that I did not want them, I'd begun to question whether I meant it. I'd said the same about not wanting to marry, and my husband was the single most fortunate choice in my life. I did not want to make a decision about children by avoiding making one, a path older friends had chosen and warned against.

My husband knew of my anxieties about this and other issues, and as I look back on those days I still remember a question he asked. It should have been relatively innocuous. "Who are the women you know who are happy?" he asked. I felt my chest tighten. After a longer than usual pause I answered, "I don't like to use the word happy." The word did not sound thoughtful, I said, adding that I preferred "satisfied." But I knew I was stalling, unwilling to own up to the questions really racing through my mind. If I couldn't think of any happy women off the top of my head, what did that mean for me? I'd recently read a biography of Alva Myrdal—a Nobel laureate, author and mother—and had been surprised when she characterized the major quest of her life: "How do I become myself?" Would I ever know the answer?

Although I was not fully conscious of it when I narrowed my list of women to Meredith, Rachael, and Alison, I see now that I focused on them because each represented different parts of my own anxieties and wishes, my worries and hopes about how to live my life. "Madame Bovary, c'est moi," Flaubert once said of his heroine, and I could say the same of Alison, Rachael, and Meredith. I was taking my own conflicts and filtering their answers through my own life. Alison represented the independent and autonomous yearnings in me—a woman identified solely by her own accomplishments, who did not need a child to complete her life. Meredith reflected the nurturer in me, who wanted to believe a woman could have meaningful work and mother her children without passing them off completely to someone else's care. Rachael fell in the middle and mirrored my ambivalence.

Over the years our discussions had fallen into a pattern. After I asked my questions, the women would ask me questions. For example, Rachael asked me several times if it bothered me that my husband said the decision to have a child was ultimately mine and not his. That was a copout, she insisted. I told her I disagreed, but I had learned enough from the process so that I needed to listen carefully to my answers to see if I had withheld important truths from myself, revelations that would wash over me with the shock of cold water. If Rachael could say out loud that she was confused and could reexamine her premises, so should I.

What was the nature of my own conflict? I knew I would never feel comfortable making a decision about children until I first understood it. I eliminated two factors quickly. My hesitation wasn't based on not liking children or child activity. I had a stepdaughter I'd loved since she was 3 and I was 22, and one of my great delights as a young woman had been revisiting with her favorite childhood books and movies and finding an excuse to drive out to the petting farm or tromp through a pumpkin field. I also did not worry about recreating a difficult maternal relationship, as did Rachael, Meredith, and Alison. To the contrary, my relationship with my mother has always given me deep and abiding comfort.

The most obvious obstacles were my practical anxieties. A loss of physical freedom was one factor, as was the potential disruption to our marriage. Having lived together for more than a dozen years, we had an intense intimacy that I feared losing. These, I thought, were all important concerns, but not enough. I forced myself to probe further. At the heart of my anxiety was a deeper fear. I worried about losing myself, the vision of the person I thought I wanted to be. I'd always wanted to write, but most of the women writers I admired did not have children. If they did, they were able to write very little, partly from fatigue and partly from a sense of drift. I was

277

a nurturing person—a giver—and I worried that if I had children they would become my focus, perhaps my only focus, and my excuse to avoid risk. I'd seen other women hide themselves in their children, wrapping their identities tighter and tighter into their children until they no longer existed separately, and I did not believe I would be immune. I was not a natural enough writer to believe I could glide easily to safety, whatever the bumps along the road. I needed time to myself, lots of it, to think about my work.

As I write now, I feel I have come to terms with these anxieties and myself as a woman. I am 37 and my husband and I have decided to try to have a baby, not because time is running out but because I am ready. Having listened closely to the stories of the women, I have listened even more closely to myself. Many of my anxieties are still valid, but others no longer are. My adoption of the model of the masculine artist, I see now, was based on an incomplete study of the options open to a woman and a writer. I believe I understand now what I need to do to create as a thinker and writer, as well as a woman and a wife to maintain balance in my life. I also recognize that I understand my own needs well enough to state that I desire a family beyond what I have now to extend and challenge me, not to complete me. Still, I have no fantasies that having a child will be easy. In fact, I know from Meredith it will be hard, very hard, and that there will be days when I am overwhelmed. But I also know from Meredith there will also be days when I will wonder why I did not have a child earlier. I still have many anxieties, but I believe I know now how to overcome, or at least control them. I will be vigilant—protecting what I have while carefully seeking more.

In closing with my own life my aim is not to engage in an exercise in confessional journalism. Rather, I hope, my small example demonstrates the value of listening to the unvarnished stories of other women's lives. I was concerned about making a decision about having a child, and listening to others forced me to listen more carefully to myself. Other women may find themselves wondering whether they should marry or divorce, change jobs or move. I believe most woman can gain something from these three stories, if it is only comfort and consolation that they are not alone in what they have felt and experienced. To transform the present, a woman must first give voice to the past. That is her hope for the future, and her responsibility.

Acknowledgments

When it comes to writing books, journalists are luckier than most because they can call on friends who share their habit, or their interest. I was assisted throughout my work on this book by the help, good counsel, and encouragement of numerous people.

David Greenberg, now the managing editor of *The New Republic*, devoted endless hours to this book. He brought more clarity to my writing and more rigor to my thinking. His handiwork is on every page, and his spirit embedded in my heart. I am eternally indebted to him.

I next thank my editors at *The Washington Post*, who graciously granted me a leave and then extended it several times, always with understanding. Benjamin C. Bradlee, the executive editor at the start of my research, is peerless as a journalist and a friend. Leonard Downie, his successor, and Robert Kaiser, the managing editor, are the top newspapermen of the *Post*'s new generation. They too always encouraged me. Milton Coleman, the assistant managing editor for the metropolitan staff at the *Post*, was the best friend a writer could have—he was patient and understanding. To them, I say a hundred thanks.

Lucy Shackelford, who has since left the *Post* for *Newsweek* magazine, never failed to find the information I requested. D'Vera Cohn, a talented writer on the metropolitan staff, gave me valuable suggestions after reading my manuscript and never once showed signs of tiring of discussing my latest ideas. Richard Cohen, the *Post* columnist and my friend, rescued me with a useful read and kind words at a time when I needed it most, as did David Maraniss, who thoughtfully read part of this book when he was busy writing his own. Steve Luxenberg, the assistant managing editor for projects at the *Post*, is my mentor in countless ways. Olwen Price was a great help. I'd also like to thank my colleagues Bill Powers, Marie Arana-Ward, Sari Horwitz, Nell Henderson, and Ben Weiser.

Richard E. Snyder was the chairman of Simon & Schuster when I began this book, and the godfather to its inception and fruition. He will always have a big place in my heart. My editor at Simon & Schuster, Laurie Bernstein, has a nimble mind and deft touch with a pencil. She performed the greatest service an editor can for a writer: sending something back when it wasn't good enough. Annie Hughes, an assistant editor there, helped at every stage. Also at Simon & Schuster I'd like to thank Carolyn K. Reidy, Michele Martin, Alice Mayhew, John Paul Jones, Rebecca Saletan, Emily Remes, Margaret Cheney, and Carin Goldberg.

Others, too, deserve special thanks. Carl Bernstein read various parts of this manuscript, and offered several helpful suggestions, as did Laura Yorke. Judy Lansing, a friend who is also a therapist, went way beyond the call of duty and read my manuscript twice. Karen Alexander cleared the deck to read and edit this manuscript. They will always have my gratitude.

Nearly all the information in this book came from my own reporting, but I consulted numerous newspaper and magazine articles. *The Washington Post, The New York Times,* and *Newsday* helped me understand Meredith Vieira's time at *60 Minutes.* I also relied on Lynn Povich's insightful interview with Meredith in *Working Woman* and Richard Valeriani's smart piece about her in *Fame. Working Mother* and *Esquire* magazines were also helpful and are cited. *The Charleston Gazette* and *The Daily Mail* covered Rachael Worby extensively and thoroughly. Sara Overton's profile in the *Sunday Gazette-Mail* merits particular mention.

Several books and authors informed my thinking. No woman should ever write without first consulting *Writing a Woman's Life* by Carolyn G. Heilbrun. I underlined sentences on almost every page. Like the best thinkers, Heilbrun makes arguments that immediately resonate as truthful because you realize you've known what she says all your life yet never quite articulated it. The poet and essayist Adrienne Rich is Heilbrun's peer with *On Lies, Secrets, and Silence,* a book I first read nearly 15 years ago, and I still marvel at its brilliance. *Toward a New Psychology of Women* by the psychiatrist Jean Baker Miller helped me understand some of the universalities of a woman's experience, as did *Our Treacherous Hearts* by Rosalind Coward. *May You Be the Mother of a Hundred*

Sons, by my *Post* colleague Elizabeth Bumiller, sat on my desk as a model.

I owe great thanks to my lawyer and agent Robert B. Barnett, who shepherded me through this project and gave me some of the best advice I received. So did Sally Quinn, the best friend around, who has helped me every step of the way since I arrived in Washington in 1980. I'd also like to thank for the special help and guidance they gave me: Joan Claybrook, Lesley Stahl, Susan Mercandetti, Ann Fishman, and Tanya Hilton.

I cannot thank my three subjects enough. They gave of their time willingly, generously, and bravely. Dozens of other people provided information for this book. I thank each one of them. I would like to single out some for particular gratitude: Thane Asch, Martha Barnitt, Gaston Caperton, Maureen Cashin, Richard Cohen (Meredith's husband), Craig Evans, Holly and Paul Fine, Michelle Friedman, Frank Gump, Don Hewitt, Andy Lack, Paul LoGerfo, Roman Nowygrod, Herbert Pardes, Jennifer Patterson, Keith Reemstma, Freya Schnabel, Suzanne St. Pierre, and Mike Wallace.

My good friends Lisa Berg, Susan Davis, and Patience O'Connor and her husband Jim Wooten propped me up many times. They are my soulmates. My sisters—Veronica, Grail, Diana, and Daria—are my closest friends, along with my brother Redmond. I am thankful for each of them every day. My stepdaughter Tali, who started college this year, was an invaluable consultant, reminding me constantly of what it means to be a woman. I miss her. Rosa Criollo is the kind of person I always want on my side. She is kind and caring. I thank her.

My mother is the finest woman I know, and she informs everything I do. One of my sisters once said my mother was her best friend. I was about to argue with her when I realized we could share this honor. I thank her every day. My father is my mother's complement. He has kept me straight and grounded throughout my life, and taught me the value of integrity and honesty. He is a principled man.

Bob Woodward, my husband, encouraged and supported me from the start. The author of seven books, he knew the drill. He read and edited many drafts, and offered numerous suggestions, every one of them helpful. He told me when something was good, but more importantly when it wasn't quite there. He gave me space and needed proximity. He was always available. I am enriched by him daily. I know of no greater gift than the love he has given me. I cherish him, adore him, and thank him.

About the Author

Elsa Walsh has been a reporter for the *Washington Post* since 1980; she currently writes for *The New Yorker*. She has won numerous journalism awards and was a finalist for the Pulitzer Prize in investigative journalism. She lives with her husband, Bob Woodward, in Washington, D.C.